187 LIVES

187 **LIVES**
A Remembrance

(With 12 pages of colour photographs)

The Indian Express Team

HarperCollins *Publishers* India

First published in India in 2008 by
HarperCollins *Publishers* India
Building No 10, Tower A, 4th Floor, DLF Cyber City, Phase II,
Gurugram – 122002
www.harpercollins.co.in

1 2 3 4 5 6 7 8 9 10

ISBN: 9788172237189

Typeset in 11.5/15 Cochin
Mindway Design Pvt. Ltd.

Contents

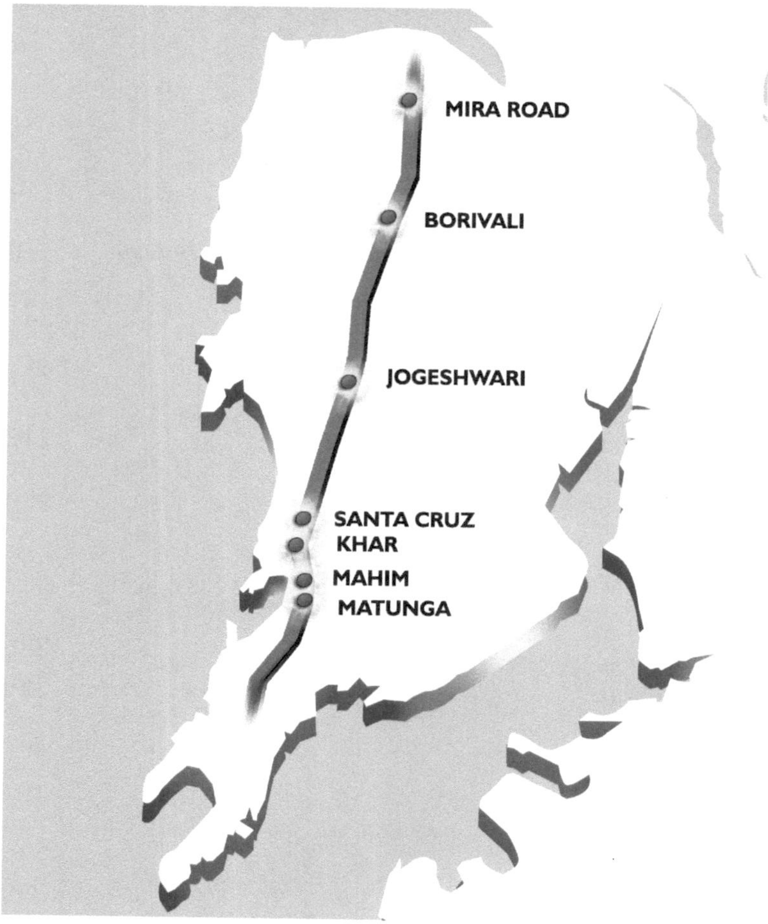
MIRA ROAD
BORIVALI
JOGESHWARI
SANTA CRUZ
KHAR
MAHIM
MATUNGA

Foreword

Shekhar Gupta

This is a book not about 187 lives lost in the Mumbai serial train blasts during the rush hour on July 11, 2006. It's about 187 lives lived in this city. And the hundreds that continue to be touched by them. This is, therefore, not a collection of obituaries, these are snapshots of hope in India's most hopeful city.

So you will read about Zubair Pathan, a 20-year-old, whose dream was to become a chartered accountant, and who always travelled first class. When his father frowned on such expensive ways, he would tug at his beard and say: 'Dada, who else will spend your money?'

Zubair was killed that evening.

Kruti Killawala's father, too.

At 18, she may be the youngest insurance agent in the country as she's working on adding to her father's clients. Why? That's what she wants to do, she says. After all, her father's papers were the one thing that survived those blasts. In a father's death, a daughter found her calling.

If terrorists tell us that they have the power to choose the way we die, the only way to fight back is by not giving them the power to change the way we live.

That's why Mumbai Life Stories.

There's another reason. And that has to do with the limitations of daily journalism. For, within hours of the blasts, as reporters of *The Indian Express* spread out across a city attacked, in homes and hospitals, the stories seemed to be flying away on different tracks.

Two women were among the dead. An overwhelming number of those who died were men who were the sole breadwinners. Families were suddenly left stranded, the death of a member an anchor that had suddenly given way. Police and security agencies had thrown a security net across the city, were picking up suspects both usual and unusual.

While these were the stories of the days and the nights that followed, we realized there was one story that was falling between the dots we were struggling to join. It wasn't a conventional news story, it was a story about grandfathers, fathers, sons, brothers, husbands, mothers, wives, daughters, daughters-in-law and friends.

In short, 187 stories, of lives lived, of grief and hope, of picking up the pieces and building all over again.

Of Hemlata Yadav, 19, who had recently joined the Home Guards and was looking to apply for a government job to help send her brother to an English-medium school.

Of Pratik Patil, 18, working hard to be the big boy in his home. He got caught on the wrong train while going to check if his younger sister had got admission in her new college.

Of Ashok Vaghela, 40, the accountant who had finally got his tiny piece of the Mumbai dream: the family had moved out of their chawl to a flat in Borivali.

Of Yogesh Futane, 26, who was working on his MBA through the tears of losing his two-month-old son to malaria.

Of Chandrakanth Mithani, 65, a new grandfather.

Of Aejaz Sheikh, 41, whose high-point of the day would come at midnight when he would return from work and chat with his ten-year-old daughter.

And of Salim Kundiwala, 42, the free spirit, who was saving to take his mother on the Haj pilgrimage.

Sons, brothers, fathers and daughters. Mumbai was their

place of death, it didn't matter what was their place of birth.

This needs to be underlined at a time when our politicians manufacture debates about who is a Mumbaiite: the one born in the city or the one who walked out a railway train from Lucknow last week, the one who celebrates Chhat Puja in Chowpatty or the one who doesn't.

When we began documenting each life lost in the Mumbai train blasts, our team of reporters took it up as a journalistic challenge but soon realized that it went beyond what they had ever worked on. The search for an address – many a time the wrong one was printed in the police's list of dead – followed up by meeting the traumatized family. Listening to them recall moments of lives that would never return. Going back to check a fact, a name, a number. Speaking to friends and colleagues. Trying to piece together a life lived through a death. There were days when we had reporters coming back in tears, driven to exhaustion by the sheer emotional weight of the assignment. Yet, while they took a break, another got on the job. Because these stories had to be told. There was no way out.

Readers from across the world responded. One said she felt comfort in the grief, that the stories told her how lucky and privileged she was. Another reader from the United States read that a father had promised his child a bicycle before he died. She helped the child get one. Thousands contributed to *The Indian Express's* My Mumbai Trust. And at a moving function held this year, the funds were distributed to many families.

This book also looks beyond the lives lost, into the worlds of those who lost everything but their lives – the survivors, like Parag Sawant, whose crippling head injury has left him permanently befuddled, a condition in which his infant daughter's comprehension is already more developed than his; or 22-year-old Amit Singh, once a passionate volleyball player, whose limbs are frozen lifeless, but whose eyes hold a flicker of hope.

It explores the lives of those who lost their husbands and the support and courage they try to lend each other by meeting whenever they can; it looks at the robust Mumbai rail, that transports six million people a day, weary, battle-worn, much maligned and yet the city's lifeline.

From the victims to the alleged perpetrators, this book also gives an update on the investigation into the blasts, the manner in which the suspects involved were rounded up, and a summary of their trial in court so far.

And of course, even in this, a chronicle of the dead, it celebrates the indefatigable spirit of Mumbai – and its life.

Postscript:

As this book was going to press, came the news of the death of Ashfaq Khan, 54, an electric engineer with the railways, who was seriously injured in the blasts and had since undergone seven brain surgeries. The father of twin girls, he was partially paralyzed and had suffered some loss of memory before losing the battle for his life. Khan was in the first class compartment of a Borivali local when the blast ripped through near Santa Cruz station. 'He was not the same person after the blasts,' said his wife Rubina. 'Sometimes he forgot me and the house but he never forgot our twins, Sadaf and Saman. He wanted to get them to study as much as they could.'

The 188th story, an echo of the 187 Lives.

Mumbai Rail

Amrita Shah

The Mumbai Metropolitan Region is the fifth largest metropolitan region in the world. It occupies an area of 4355 square kilometres and has an estimated population of 19.7 million people. Within this sprawling region, studded with hills, water bodies and independent townships, is a smaller entity, jutting out like a shoehorn at the edge of India's western coastline, known as Greater Mumbai. This entity, covering 468 square kilometres, comprises the island city and its suburbs on the eastern and the western flank. Within Greater Mumbai, occupying the southern half thrusting into the Arabian Sea, is Mumbai city, the few square miles comprising some of the world's most expensive real estate, which offers more jobs than any other comparably sized space in the country, which is talked of as being on par with the global centres of the world, and which has been mythologized in films, books and popular songs as the 'city of dreams'.

It is difficult to imagine how this vast, unwieldy region is traversed; what is the link that unites its disparate parts? And what is the driving force that provides mobility and matches demand with supply across such distances? One answer to these questions can be found in what has become an iconic picture of Mumbai. It is a photograph of a local train with passengers balancing atop the roof, clinging to the sides like lizards, spilling out of the doors. It is an image which suggests that Mumbai, India's financial powerhouse and emerging global city, still runs on a relic of the past.

The Mumbai Suburban Railway System is Asia's oldest railway system, variously described, in strikingly visceral terms, as the city's 'lifeline', its 'veins', its 'spine'. Run by two zonal railways, Western and Central, operating 2226 train services, comprising 191 rakes and run by Electric Multiple Units (EMUs) across 319 route kilometres, this is one of the most extensive urban train networks in the world. It is also the most crowded, carrying a daily load of 6.3 million passengers – twice the number that use London's Underground, six times the daily traffic on Berlin's U-Bahn and substantially more than the 4.5 million that use all of New York's public transport.

The Mumbai Suburban Railway consists of the Western, Central and the Harbour Lines. On a map, the tracks, like bunched-up electric cables, unravel along the bumpy coastline or fork eastward into the hinterland. From the downtown centre with its sea-lapped towers, the tracks thrust into the jostling back-end of everyday life, the names of stations along the way – Santa Cruz, Dahisar, King's Circle, Ambernath, Panvel – conjuring up evocative images of the past and present.

The trains, popularly known as 'locals', are rakes with basic, open carriages and hard wooden seats in most of the compartments. The walls are flaky and scratched, the floors dirty, and the grills on the windows a necessary protection against chain snatchers and stone throwers. Coaches are specially reinforced to take additional loads: rakes with a capacity for 1700 passengers carry 4500 passengers at peak hour resulting in a 'super dense crush load' of 14 to16 standing passengers per square metre of floor space. Despite these constraints it is a marvellously punctual, efficient and quick system operating a service every few minutes and running long hours from 4 am to 1 am, seven days a week.

Indeed, the evolution of Mumbai from a fledgling port and textile town in the late 1800s to its status as a twenty-first century commercial behemoth might not have been possible without the hardy resourcefulness of the Mumbai Suburban Railway System. The very first train, rolled out of Boribunder, heading for Thane in 1853. Over the decades that followed, a full-fledged Suburban system was established, an event that co-incided with the growth of Mumbai beyond the colonial fort walls to the newly developed Dadar–Matunga–Wadala–Sion neighbourhood in 1899 in the east and suburbs such as Mahim, Bandra and Juhu in the west in the 1930s. Mumbai's linear shape and the concentration of employment in the southernmost part of the island made it particularly suited to train travel in comparison to cities like Kolkata and Bangalore where buses were the preferred option.

An extensive network of tracks had been laid in the initial phase of development but as the city's population increased – rising by as much as 40 per cent according to some estimates in the late 1900s – residents were pushed further and further away from the island city and the Suburban Railway System expanded its services to accommodate the increased demand. Between 1992 and 2005, increased connectivity between the island city and the hinterland and within the hinterland boosted, at long last, the development of Navi Mumbai, a twin city on the mainland planned way back in the seventies with the aim of decongesting Mumbai.

The increase in commuting time, with many traversing as many as 120 kilometres a day by train, has lent the local trains the flavour of a home away from home. In the body of the beast is a world on wheels. It is here that the unburdening of hearts takes place; where a gambling den emerges from two window seats and a briefcase; where an idol in the brake van marks the annual passage of Ganesha; where vegetables are sliced for dinner; where handlebars are swung by monkey-faced schoolboys; where furtive glances lead to marriages or in some cases, broken marriages; where newspapers are read and discarded; where the last bit of homework is hurried through; where sweaters are knitted for those still waiting to arrive in the world, and where the end is often imminent: on an ordinary day an average of thirteen people are fated to meet their death, falling off a train, electrocuted by overhead electric wires or crushed while illegally crossing the tracks.

Hawkers bring the market into the trains: fragrant gajras, recycled notebooks, frilly nightgowns, cheap toys, cell phone covers, last month's magazines and crunchy samosas. The nasal lament of young boys trained by an underground school of beggar-musicians passes through the compartments resuscitating forgotten film songs. It is a hard life they sing of. A hard life that the trains know of, taking fresh blood in the mornings, carrying tired souls in the evenings.

Unlike in urban centres of the west, where a boost in mobility enhanced social stratification with people of means moving to the suburbs at the turn of the last century, the Mumbai locals provide evidence of a more even distribution of socio-economic classes. On any given day, a varied stream of passengers passes through the trains: office-goers, businessmen, eager schoolchildren, stockbrokers in the late mornings, street-walkers returning home on the night train, fisherwomen with their *tokris* of silver fish.

The excessive reliance on the local trains, however, has extracted a price. Crimes, particularly against women, have become more frequent. And between 1992 and 2005 over 15 incidents of mob violence occurred over delays and rescheduling of trains.

With the rapid makeover of urban centres all over the country and the implementation of an urban transport plan for Mumbai, however, it is likely that these problems will be addressed, partly by refurbishing the Suburban System itself and partly with the introduction of other transportation systems such as the metro rail, sea-links and water transportation systems.

Regardless of what changes the future may bring, the Mumbai 'Local' will live on, for, in its reliability, its sturdiness and its resilience it has always been more than a means of getting from one place to another.

It is emblematic of the very spirit of Mumbai.

7/11

Swatee Kher

For over six million residents of bustling Mumbai city, planning their working day involves synchronizing their time schedules with that of the city's lifeline. The nine-coach and twelve-coach trains transport residents, many from far-off suburbs, to the business districts in South Mumbai every morning, and bring them back to their homes each night. That Tuesday morning I was more than happy to be able to avoid the trains – packed, as always, to the point of spilling over – as it was my day off.

Waiting at the railway station in the morning to catch a train to work, a friend had called to complain about delays and rains. As the train finally chugged in, she hung up hurriedly saying, 'Got to fight my way in, I'll call later.' She didn't call me after that, and I gathered her 'fight' – the mad scramble to get into the train, to wrest a seat if you are very lucky, or even to get a place to stand peacefully without being squashed and pushed – had occupied her completely. With her 9 to 5 job, she travels during the busiest hours of the service.

That evening, as news of the blasts started to gain momentum, I tried frantically to contact her, but couldn't. All the communication networks were down and passengers were stranded in the middle of nowhere as Mumbai's railway network ground to a halt. As it became clearer with every passing minute that Mumbai had just suffered another serial bomb blast – the only city in the world to witness serial bomb blasts twice – I couldn't help thinking the thought which, these days, the average Mumbaiite has begun increasingly to entertain: that in this city, there is no longer any guarantee that a person who leaves his home in the morning will return home at night.

I raced down to Borivali Railway Station – minutes from my residence – as soon as I heard the news. Rumours of two blasts were doing the rounds. Dazed commuters were spilling onto the main road as police, NGOs, and political party workers tried to control and organize the hysterical crowd. Entry points into the railway station had been cordoned off, except for two from which ambulances and taxis sped the injured to the nearby Bhagwati hospital. Opposite the main entrance of Borivali station repeated public announcements by the police attempted to pacify the public and establish order, a task made doubly difficult by the breakdown of the city's mobile telephone networks. Panicked passengers, unable to make contact with their loved ones, were growing more and more frantic. Confusion and chaos reigned all around, bringing back similar memories of the floods that had hit Mumbai in 2005.

After gathering the details of the blast in Borivali from senior police officials at the station, I set off for a night at the civic hospital. At Bhagwati hospital, the narrow corridor was teeming with anxious people searching for missing loved ones, the fear that their lives had changed irrevocably writ large on their faces. Doctors, nurses, policemen, volunteers raced about shouting orders, giving crucial life-saving emergency treatment, as the number of the injured and the dead increased by the minute. Hundreds of people crowded outside the casualty room, scanning the names being added continually on the lists put up on black boards. College students and residents from nearby areas were helping trace patients in the general wards, as relatives crowded outside.

In a matter of hours, the OPD and social service room had been converted into a makeshift morgue, as 47 bodies were laid out haphazardly, almost one over the other, awaiting identification. Outside this room, I met a lady who had rushed here from Vile Parle with her husband, who feared his brother was among the victims. I kept her company while her husband went in to scan the bodies. She spoke to me urgently, giving me the details of her life – fears, hopes, wishes, opinions – as if suddenly aware how meaningless these all were on the brink of becoming. There was an intimacy to our conversation that is seldom felt between strangers. I tried to assuage her fears but felt quite helpless in the face of a tragedy whose mammoth scale was becoming more apparent by the minute.

I moved away from her and spoke to a former crime branch official attached to Borivali Police Station who remarked that it was the worst sight he had seen in his entire career. There was no let-up in the numbers of the wounded being wheeled into hospital. Another official spoke tersely about vital clues they had picked up on the perpetrators and their modus operandi.

Checking the morgue before I left for filing my story, I met the woman who'd spoken to me earlier. She said their worst fears had been confirmed; her brother-in-law was among the dead. Her husband had identified his body by its toenails – there was no other familiar feature left on his scorched and mangled corpse with which to identify him. She held me tight and said she did not know how to face her family. I left as they were finishing the police formalities.

Then the cell phones came back on and I spoke to friends and colleagues stranded at stations, hospitals and offices – all safe – except for the friend who had called me from the station in the morning. I still had no news of her. By now the streets had been cleared of the crowds and volunteers waiting at junctions to help people catch buses. At home, television images made explicit the devastating impact of the blasts.

Another hour or so later, and now the railway station wore an eerie, desolate look – only the policemen and railway engineers were left, scavenging through the rubble. They were busy at work at the spot of the blast on platform four. A tea-stall owner recounted his version of the minutes immediately before and after the blast, as I watched the devastated railway compartment being searched by sniffer dogs. The anti-terrorist squad was gathering evidence and looking for any clues the bombers might have left. I met Prince, the four-year-old, black Labrador, who'd had an exhausting couple of hours searching out explosive material at the blast sites in Bandra, Khar and Jogeshwari. I was shown pieces of RDX that the team had collected from the train.

Then I went back to the hospital. By morning, most of the injured had been united with their loved ones. Among those still unidentified, facing this terrible ordeal without the support of a caring family member by his side, was a ten-year-old boy who lay quietly in the intensive care unit with stitches on his face. After we wrote his story, and television broke it the next day, help poured in for the boy from all quarters. But there was still no trace of his parents. Three days later, relatives turned up from Panvel after having seen his picture in newspapers.

Meanwhile, that night, there was still no news of my friend. She called finally in the early hours of the next morning – talking of delays and trains and her inability to communicate with anyone. As she recounted her horrific experiences of the night before, I thanked God she was among the lucky ones – able, at least, to tell her tale.

INTO THE LONG NIGHT

The Indian Express Mumbai Bureau

Even at the best of times, there's one scene that never changes in Mumbai: battered railway coaches packed with the human flotsam of a brutal city. Men, women, and children, travelling like refugees, to do the only thing they know: survive. Mumbai's Western Railway line, the fragile umbilical cord that links the metropolis to the motherland, across the amniotic swell of the Arabian Sea is also Mumbai's lifeline, ferrying six million citizens from the suburbs to the congested heart of the city.

On Tuesday, July 11, 2006, that lifeline was savagely severed by a hand that obviously knew Mumbai's anatomy well. Seven serial bombs went off at seven stations – all key nerve centres – in peak-hour traffic. When in doubt, aim for the jugular. Hannibal Lecter couldn't have done better.

It wasn't the first time Mumbai was mortally wounded. In 1993, 13 bombs brought India's feisty financial capital to its knees. Back then, the prime target was the Stock Exchange, that impudent icon of progress and prosperity. The aim: to symbolically cripple a newborn economy, taking its first baby steps towards globalization.

This time the target was a much more priceless asset: the ordinary men and women of Mumbai. No wonder. After all, the Mumbaiite is, in all probability, the most hardy specimen known to mankind. A species smelted in the furnace of privation, a people who have got used to living – no, thriving – in hell. From dodging lethal potholes, sidestepping broken pavements, circumventing decomposing refuse, commuting like refugees, waking up at ungodly hours to fill buckets with water before the municipal pipelines run dry, drinking jaundiced water, watching shanties come up for free outside matchbox-sized apartments, sweating to pay off an astronomical loan for a home that may collapse the following monsoon...

It began like any ordinary day.

Seated on a platform bench, Hemlata Yadav, 19, discussed with her sister Suman Yadav and friend Madhuri how to apply for a new job. All three young girls were with a unit of the Brihanmumbai Home Guards, deployed to protect the city's woman commuters. As the girls animatedly discussed their career options the Virar-bound Fast pulled in, its first class coach just a few steps from the bench where Hemlata sat…

On his way back from computer classes in Worli, Pratik was to check the admissions list put up at Vartak College, Vasai, for his sister, Prateema, who has just cleared her Class X exams. Young and dutiful, Pratik was doing what any decent boy would do; saving his father an errand, looking out for his sister…

Every day, before leaving office at 5.15 pm, Ranjan Naik would call his wife to find out if she needed anything from town. 'That was our little ritual,' she said. But on that day she didn't have a wish-list. She just wanted her husband home in time for the Guru Purnima puja. 'We're waiting for you,' she said…

'Are you sure I need this?' M.B. Srinivas Rao protested smilingly when his wife Lakshmi handed him a men's fairness and anti-wrinkle cream to try and hide some of the scars of ageing that were gradually appearing on her 'smart and good-natured' husband of 33 years...

Chetan spoke to his mother around noon and promised to complete a family ritual to mark his father's eighth death anniversary, a date he'd missed two days ago. Around 5.15 pm, he called his wife Bhavna asking her to reach home early. In less than half an hour, both were on different trains headed to the same destination – their Borivali home...

That was the last their family members heard from their dear ones.

Terror struck Mumbai's lifeline seven times in a period of 11 minutes when the first class compartments of local trains to the city's western suburbs were wrecked by powerful blasts on July 11, 2006. At least 150 people were killed outright and over 600 injured. The blasts occurred at Mahim, Bandra, Matunga, Borivali, Mira Road, Jogeshwari and Khar. They came just hours after suspected Lashkar-e-Toiba militants had killed eight people, six of them tourists, in a series of grenade attacks in Srinagar.

Railway traffic on the Western line – the busiest of the three lines used by commuters to travel to and from work – was at its peak, with lakhs of commuters returning home when the bombs went off. The first blast occurred on a train between Khar and Santa Cruz stations, another at exactly the same time on a train near Bandra. These were followed by explosions on trains at Jogeshwari, Mahim, Mira Road, Matunga and Borivali stations. All the blasts took place inside first class compartments, ripping them apart.

Train services on the Western line were completely suspended, all trains leaving Mumbai were stopped and a red alert was sounded in the city and the rest of the state. Phone lines all over the city were choked.

At Matunga station, the blast was so powerful that it not only destroyed the first class coach but also blew off a portion of the platform roof. Bodies were seen scattered on the tracks while many of the injured, some of them profusely bleeding, were attended to by fellow travellers on the platform before being rushed to nearby hospitals.

As the blasts ripped apart train compartments elsewhere, mangled bodies of passengers were hurled out of the trains even as the survivors, many of them grievously wounded, scrambled to get out.

A short distance from Dadar station, Lower Parel was chaotic as panic gripped commuters on the platform and traffic choked the main road outside. Since all Western Railway Locals had ceased to operate following the serial blasts along the train line, most of the commuters began to make a beeline for taxis and buses outside the station.

Three of the terror blasts which rocked the city during rush hour saw the maximum casualties. At Mahim Junction Railway Station alone, the blast left at least 30 dead and another 40 injured. At the adjoining Matunga Road Railway Station at least 35 were critically injured. Both the blasts went off one after the other: 6.15 at Mahim on a train that was going towards Borivali, 6.20 at Matunga on a train that was going towards Churchgate. The third bomb, planted on a Borivali-bound train, went off as the train was approaching Santa Cruz Railway Station. Here, too, more than 30 people were injured.

At Mahim station, the first rescuers were survivors on the train and those passengers waiting at the platforms. Local residents too joined in, rescuing the injured and taking out bodies. Emergency vehicles of the Mumbai Police, the Mumbai Fire Brigade, the Brihanmumbai Corporation, and voluntary organizations also swung into action.

'I was lucky to have escaped the blast as I was in the other part of the first class compartment. I witnessed at least 25 bodies being piled up on the platform,' said Bharat Desai, a resident of Borivali. 'The train was about to leave the railway station when the blast happened. For the first two minutes we didn't know what was going on. Then we saw the compartment more than half blown away and realized it was a blast,' recalled Vijay Gandhi, a resident of Dahisar.

Local residents chipped in with food and water and makeshift stretchers. At Santa Cruz, relief and rescue work was hampered by the fact that the approach to the railway station is through congested and narrow by-lanes. However, police teams barricaded the entry and exit points to allow rescue vehicles to move in and out more speedily.

The stations were strewn with the dead and dying. Immediately and out of nowhere, anonymous men appeared to help cart the mutilated bodies away from the wreckage. '*Jo mila wohi leke aana tha*,' said Santosh Teli, who runs a private ambulance service. Quite matter-of-fact, he said he picked up whatever lay on railway platforms at Matunga and Mahim stations – bodies swathed in white, mutilated bodies, and dismembered body parts still waiting for a shroud. 'No doctor, madam,' he said when asked if paramedics were accompanying ambulances to accident sites. 'What do you need a doctor for if you've to pick up a dead body?'

Teli and others like him worked till two in the morning, ferrying the dead and injured to hospital. While dozens of ambulances reached KEM and Sion hospitals, the suburban hospitals also saw an army of autorickhaw and taxi-drivers pitching in, compassionately waiving fares for frantic Mumbaiites out searching for missing family members.

At KEM hospital, the Class IV workers returned to work even though duty hours were over. Temporary worker

Ramanand Singh laboured until 3 am, carrying body after body – 22 of them – into the narrow mortuary. 'He collapsed after that and was on a saline drip,' said a colleague. 'But he got back to work the next morning.'

Teli, who has been running his ambulance service for 12 years, remembers many tragedies – the time when the Bhoiwada police called him to rush to Chinchpokli station when a train had derailed; dozens of house collapses; accidents and sundry assignments – but nothing of this magnitude. 'Like this?' he shudders. 'Never. And, hopefully, never again.'

Hospital authorities in the city confirmed the arrival of over 100 bodies by 8:30 pm, while an unconfirmed number of injured commuters were being treated in various government and private hospitals in different parts of the city. Heavy rain, barely an hour after the explosions, affected rescue operations.

Confusion and panic gripped commuters who got stuck after train services on the Western Railway line were stopped. The Police Commissioner urged people to use the Central Railway line. The government also pressed additional buses into service, but the roads were choked till late in the evening. Looking around nervously at Churchgate station at 7.45 pm on Tuesday, Amit Narayan, 17, saw a sea of people whose minds he could read in an instant. *'How do I get home? Are my loved ones safe?'* That one thought made them all kindred souls, he says.

Luckily, an announcement at Churchgate said those looking for a roof for the night could head to the University of Mumbai's International Students' House, a hostel with a capacity of 123 students. Over 700 people spent the night there, thanking the officials profusely as they sat down to a simple but much needed meal of dal-chawal-sabzi and congregated in front of a television set. 'Those stranded, in need of a meal, or any other assistance came in,' said Dr P.C. Warke, warden of the hostel and head of the Law Department of the University of Mumbai. 'I told the canteenwallah to prepare food for everyone – there were NGOs sponsoring the costs later.'

An enormous number of mattresses and dozens of sheets materialized as if out of nowhere. The hungry kept showing up until 3 am.

Elsewhere, municipal schools opened their gates, offices at the World Trade Centre gave employees from nearby establishments space to spend the night and South Mumbai families descended on the roads with food packets, bananas, biscuits and water bottles. 'And words of support,' says Narayan. 'That was really touching.'

'Can you take the cell phone out of my pocket? I want to talk to my wife,' Mahesh Ponda asked a doctor at Sion hospital. The doctor fished out the blood-soaked cell phone from his right pocket and asked for the number. After several attempts, he managed to get through and handed over the phone to him. '*Saru che*,' Mahesh reassured his wife, his hand shaking as he held the phone. What he didn't tell her was that splinters had pierced his left hand and abdomen. He had a one-and-a-half centimetre deep gash in his stomach which the doctors had stitched up.

Mahesh and his friend, also called Mahesh, had boarded the train at Dadar for Borivali. 'The train arrived at 6.04 pm. We boarded the first class compartment. After five minutes or so, between Matunga and Mahim, I heard a deafening sound. I thought a fan had fallen but suddenly the roof split open. I fell, I don't remember what happened after that.'

At Sion hospital, not far from the scene of the blasts at Matunga and Khar stations, the rain water acquired a red hue as the injured were brought in. Kishore Jain (48) was in the first class compartment of the 5.57 pm Fast to Virar when the blast occurred near Matunga station. As he sat with a bandaged arm, waiting for his son Ashish to pick him up from outside Ward 3 of the Casualty and Emergency Department, he said, 'There was a very loud noise and smoke filled the compartment. I saw the man next to me, he was bleeding from the ear. My arm hurt, there were splinters all over, but I managed to walk till Matunga station and came here in a police van.'

Padam Gandhi, who was also in the same compartment, stood near Jain but was too shaken to talk about what happened. Khem Chand, a plastic merchant from Matunga, who brought Gandhi to the hospital in a taxi, recalled the scene: 'My workers and I rushed to the station when we heard the bang. We split into groups of two and threes and tried to take care of the injured. I saw this man standing in bloodstained clothes, looking absolutely dazed,' said Chand, still trying to calm Gandhi.

As the dead were being carried away and the stranded commuters being looked after, another monumental task needed immediate attention. The railways had to be up and running again. Fire extinguishers in hand, seven motor men and seven guards joined relief efforts, then kept an all-night vigil around the mangled train compartments, hungry and tired, until the rakes were safely inside car-sheds the next morning.

Next, they had to get the railway service up and running again. General Manager Rajkamal Rao was not even in Mumbai, but he got on the phone and planned everything along with Additional General Manager Vivek Sahai, an experienced hand who had been divisional railway manager of Central Railway when the Mulund blast occurred in March 2003. They chalked out plans to the last detail—who would be at the control room, who would coordinate things at the sites, how the inspection of the sites would be carried out, everything.

'It was team work,' said Sahai. 'Everybody played an important role, whether an official or a D-grade employee.'

Police permission was needed to remove the damaged compartments from the tracks. A team of gang-men and points-men examined the entire railway track, a tower wagon fitted with gas cutters and other repair equipment was kept ready on the fifth line at Virar, Vasai Road, Andheri and Mumbai Central stations.

Every field officer and employee was immediately called to report for duty. Chief Mechanical Engineer S.C. Agarwal got the workshop opened past midnight— as more coaches and equipment had to be fetched. Through the night, Divisional Railway Manager (Western Railway) Satya Prakash monitored the progress from the Mumbai Central control room.

At 11 pm, when Rajkamal Rao reached Mumbai by car, he saw his line's local trains were back on track. '5000 railway workers were rushed to the affected areas. Our senior officials camped in control rooms at Churchgate and Mumbai Central through the night,' he said.

Sixteen hours after the terrible blasts in the Mumbai locals, the line was fully restored

Candle-light vigils, mohalla committee meetings, *shraddhanjalis*, condolence meetings, and finally, public dialogue. From students and professionals to social workers and policemen, Mumbai was trying to do everything to ensure that the cosmopolitan heart of the country did not burn in the wake of the serial blasts.

'One spark, that's all it takes to provoke a communal incident,' said Shakeel Ahmed of the Nirbhay Bano Andolan, a social organization working for communal harmony. The activists were not the only ones who knew this – after all the riots after the Godhra incident had left 793 Muslims and 293 Hindus dead, according to official figures. So Mumbai's peace soldiers were busy, keeping religion-based animosity at bay.

Activist Teesta Setalvad's Citizens for Justice and Peace (CJP) – formed in the aftermath of the Gujarat riots – planned a mass contact programme in trains and among citizens, to assuage fears and suspicions.

Small public meetings across the island city, especially in communally sensitive areas like Mira Road and Bhayander, were also on the cards. Meanwhile, social workers like S.S. Sanjeev were mobilizing locals with the message of communal harmony. 'Local representatives from traditionally riot-prone areas are getting together,' said Sanjeev.

In fact, in the by-lanes of Jogeshwari, and areas like Meghwadi and Gandhinagar, local citizens cut across religious barriers and enlisted their support to the police; they even submitted a memorandum seeking that political parties be restrained from provoking violence.

Behind it all was a single idea: to de-polarize communal tension. It was imperative that Mumbai stay peaceful despite the blasts. After all, the last thing the people of Mumbai wanted was to add to the heavy price paid by 187 lives.

187 **LIVES**

(The following stories are arranged in the order that this series first appeared in *The Indian Express*)

Hemlata Yadav

Home Guard, worked to help pay brother's school fees

The only photograph the Yadavs have of their daughter Hemlata (19) is the passport-sized one she had got taken when she dropped out of school to give herself and her family a second shot at a better future in this city, by joining the Brihanmumbai Home Guards. Seated on a platform bench in Borivali station with her sister Suman and a friend, all three of them colleagues, Hemlata was discussing a new job when the Virar-bound Fast pulled in – its first class coach stopping just a few feet away from the bench where she sat. The impact of the bomb threw all of them to the floor. 'Madhuri and I fell to the ground from the bomb's impact but my sister was injured badly. I tried to pick her up but her right side was wounded. She never got up. Guddu was the more outgoing one of us. She was working hard to send our brother to school. She dreamt of getting a government job and resuming her studies on the side,' Suman remembers sadly. Hemlata's immediate superior, Zonal Commandant Vasudev Yogi recalls, 'The uniform held great appeal for her. In her year's service during Gokul Ashtami and then over the past eight months at the railway station, she was always calm, composed. She would definitely have got a good job in the government or the police.' Her mother Sumitra remembers the things her daughter loved, the good things, and the bad, but most especially, she remembers that Tuesday's unfulfilled promise: 'She loved arbi. On Tuesday morning, she went out to purchase some and told me she would cook it herself for the family when she returned home after work...'

PRATIK PATIL

A responsible elder brother and computer whiz

On Terrible Tuesday, Pratik was doing the things an elder brother usually does – saving his father an errand; looking out for his sister. On his way back from computer class in Worli, Pratik Patil was to check the admissions list put up at Vartak College, Vasai, for his sister Prateema who had just cleared her Class X exam. He did, but couldn't reach home in faraway Nallasopara to tell them that her name was on it. To his teenaged sister and brother Sachin he was their best friend. To his parents, father Nivrutti and mother Sangeeta he was the 'responsible one'. For himself, a geek in the making, all Pratik wanted was to be a part of the new workforce of young ambitious talent that had propelled India and its IT sector onto the world map. 'Why would I say anything to him? He was doing all that was needed, be it helping at home or studies. There was never any reason to complain,' says his homemaker mother, recalling how, after he'd completed Class XII, they had to dissuade him from taking a job with Taj Hotels to help support the family. Only last year, Pratik had assembled a computer for himself. 'Naturally, he was very possessive about it. When he was away at his grandmother's for 20 days, he locked it up. It was only after he came back that we asked him to open it for his brother to play on,' says his father. His mother remembers what Pratik said when his class XII results were announced: 'He came home and told me his friends were asking for sweets. Then he said he would give them sweets once Prateema's results were out. "We'll give sweets together to everyone," he'd said.'

Ranjan Naik

ITI officer, his young son was the centre of his life.

Sandhya Naik will blame herself for a long time. Every day, before he left office at 5.15 pm, her husband Ranjan Naik would call to find out if she needed anything from town. 'That was our little ritual,' she says. But on Terrible Tuesday, she only wanted him home early for the Guru Purnima puja. He couldn't make it. The blast in the first class coach of the Virar Local killed him. 'Had I asked him to get something, he wouldn't have been on that train,' frets Sandhya. For 40-year-old Ranjan Naik, a deputy manager with the Indian Telephone Industries (ITI), his eight-year-old son Jivesh (Bittu at home) was the centre of his life, says his wife, a homemaker for the last nine years. Now she has many worries: 'I've heard they will recruit people only as Class IV employees. I'm a graduate but I don't even mind a clerical post.' Her biggest worry is Bittu's education, his future. Bittu offers a solution as only an eight-year-old can: 'You can give tuitions at home, Mama.' This, he adds, will ensure she's at home, to see him off as always, when he leaves for school at 11.30 am. But Sandhya has already begun preparing him for some drastic changes in their schedule. Once she starts working, she will neither be home to see him off, nor be there to greet him when he returns home from school after 6 pm. The neighbours have offered to look after him while Sandhya is away. But Bittu still can't understand why his mother will have to 'leave' him and keeps asking his aunt about it. He even promises to be 'good' and not ask for anything, except for 'the bicycle Papa promised'.

187 MUMBAI LIFE STORIES

Rasiklal Rameshchandra Merchant

HSBC securities dealer, he infused celebration in everyday life

'Daddy was the one who planned our trips,' says daughter Hetal. 'Shimla, Manali, Darjeeling, Bangalore – he had even applied for passports under *tatkaal* because he wanted to take Mummy to Thailand next month, only her passport has still not come and he was teasing her that he would leave without her.' Even as Bharti clicks her tongue in disapproval at her daughter's revelations, she smiles through her tears and talks of the cruise her husband Rasiklal Rameshchandra Merchant (50), a senior dealer with HSBC Securities, took the family on last December. '*Pehli baar* ship *pe gaye, bahut achcha laga*,' she smiles sadly. Bharti and he had danced on board the Star *Libra*. That last dance had won them the title of Best Couple and a meal ticket to a dinner at the Taj. Rasik enjoyed life on his own terms, his love for good food and his ability to infuse celebration into ordinary things are what his friends remember him for. 'He would bring the whole building together to pray, to celebrate – whether it was Navratri or Holi,' a neighbour recalls. 'He couldn't resist the kheer and pooranpoli that Mummy made, in spite of his diabetes,' says son Jigen. Merchant joined the brokerage firm Batliwala and Karani Co. after finishing Class XII from Chinai High School, Andheri and remained the link for high-profile clients for his company after its merger with James Cable and Co., and later, its acquisition by HSBC. He was also present in the trading ring of the National Stock Exchange (NSE) when the 1993 blasts occurred. Merchantbhai had seen it all over the decades.

Salim Mohammad Kundiwala

Doston ka woh azeez tha; Salim toh bas Salim tha

Just past midnight, hours after Terrible Tuesday, Salim Mohammad Kundiwala, 'every inch of his body stitched up', asked for a piece of paper. He wrote: *'Mere liye dua karna.'* Four days later, he was dead. That full stop ended 42-year-old Salimbhai's great plans: making enough money to take his mother to Haj, starting a new life three years after separating from his wife, watching his sons do well in their studies. Alone in his Asmita Vintage Complex flat, his 65-year-old mother Kitabunisa tries to keep her mind off things by preparing the evening meal, something she had given up doing a long time ago due to ill-health. 'Salim used to cook food for me after he returned from work,' says Kitabunisa, who moved in from Central Mumbai after Salim separated from his wife. Says Salim's close friend Mohammed Irfan Sheikh: 'When I hear about the police combing Muslim neighbourhoods, I tell myself that the people who did this cannot be Muslims. Because a Muslim is someone like Salim, who respected his mother, had dreams for his sons, and wished well for his friends. Those who did this cannot be human, forget being Muslim.' Sheikh says that Salim, who graduated from Maharashtra College, was in complete sync with the heartbeat of Mumbai. 'He knew the city like the back of his hand, the various street-food marts, restaurants. He was famous among our friends for introducing us to great food.' Life, says Sheikh, was beginning to look up for his friend. 'We were even considering putting out a matrimonial for him in the coming months.'

Paresh Thakkar

Insurance consultant, passionate about securing other's lives

The conversation on the afternoon of 7/11 between insurance agent Paresh Thakkar (38) and wife Dolly followed their routine. She briefed him about the day's performance of the Sensex. 'When I told him it had risen appreciably, he was very happy and said that was good news for his clients.' Hours later, Paresh was killed in the train blast at Jogeshwari station. At the South Mumbai branch of the Life Insurance Corporation of India where Thakkar worked, V. Rao, his boss of 16 years, reflects how Thakkar swiftly developed into his 'star agent'. 'In 1991, Paresh came to me saying he wanted to become an insurance agent. Once our association started, he would come at six every morning to hand me policy documents. He was like my alarm clock. Even as we sit here, I expect his call,' says Rao. But Dolly says that that's precisely how she would like to remember her husband – passionate about his work and devoted to the families he insured. The six-foot-tall, bespectacled, and soft-spoken Thakkar epitomized the quintessential Mumbaiite: self-made, hard-working and principled. In 1995, he decided to devote himself full-time to insurance, and 11 years later was putting together a plan to set up an insurance agency that would employ eight or ten people. Daughter Mansi, ten-years-old and mature beyond her years, tells her mother to be strong, as she leaves for school. 'Paresh and I wanted only one child, and we prayed that it be a daughter,' says Dolly. 'Mansi's birth was the happiest moment of our life. I am proud our daughter has imbibed her father's resolve.'

187 MUMBAI LIFE STORIES

Mohanlal Ratanlal Shrawagi

A marketing manager known for his kindness to strangers

Those who didn't know Mohanlal Shrawagi (61) in his lifetime only need to meet his sons, Sumeet and Ameet. They're grieving, but don't overlook offering an unknown reporter stranded in the rain an umbrella and a ride to the station. Had he been alive, that's just what Shrawagi would have done. When news spread that the GM (Marketing) of Metrochem Industries Ltd. was one of those claimed by Terrible Tuesday, hundreds of people, mostly strangers, came to meet Sumeet and Ameet to tell them why they'd always remain indebted to their father. 'He was just that sort of a guy,' says Sumeet, a software engineer settled in California. 'He once walked into the house and asked Mum for a couple of my shirts,' adds Ameet. They were for the rickshawallah, whose shirt was torn. In fact, when Ameet could not find his dad at work nor get him on his cell that day he automatically assumed that Shrawagi was helping somebody else. Shrawagi's boundless energy would have him up at 6 am, feeding the pigeons, sparrows and squirrels in the compound, making tea for the household and then good-naturedly racing Ameet to get ready for work. Ameet, a chartered accountant with Citibank, always lost. Now, the watchman of the uncluttered premises in Goregaon automatically points strangers to the Shrawagis's flat. 'Saab was chairman of the housing society,' he says. A week to go for his term to end, he'd just bought saplings and had spoken to the gardener in great detail about looking after them. 'The new chairman could have done it,' says Ameet, 'but Dad was never one to shirk his duty.'

Shankar Ramdin Gupta

Vakola slum boy who went on to become Canon engineer

Shankar's story is a quintessential Mumbai story. A life full of struggle, the fruits of which he was only just beginning to enjoy. Shankar Ramdin Gupta lived in the Subhash Nagar slum at Vakolal for the first 26 years of his life. But having moved on from selling lipstick as a boy to becoming a trainee engineer with Canon, he was determined that it would not be his address for the next 26 years. Things were beginning to look up for him. Four years ago, he'd married Priyanka and with the family growing – a two-and-a-half-year-old daughter and a nine-month-old son – he had already looked at a two-room tenement in a chawl near Nallasopara. 'He had only one line for me, "You have supported me for my education, I will make sure we will see happy days,"' recalls his mother Basanti Gupta. And Shankar was striving hard. Looking after his family, helping support his elder sister's family, at times sending money to relatives in UP and even saving for his sister's wedding. All from a monthly salary of Rs 12,500. 'He was a child any parent would be proud of. As a boy, he was keenly conscious of our financial condition. We really couldn't afford it, but I put him in Happy Home School at Vakola so that he could learn English,' says Basanti. Shankar would study by candlelight and when the candle burnt out, he would seldom have another one to light. So, Shankar would look for a house that had electricity and request them to allow him to sit in a corner to study. No wonder that all the members of the Subhash Nagar slum are so proud of their 'engineer boy'.

M.B. Srinivas Rao

Smart and good-natured husband of 33 years.

'Are you sure I need this?' he asked wife Lakshmi, who had just handed him a men's fairness and anti-wrinkle cream to try and hide some of the scars of ageing that were gradually appearing on her 'smart and good-natured' husband of 33 years. Despite her powers of persuasion, it turned out that M.B. Srinivas Rao (61) didn't need the cream after all. He was on the Borivali Fast when the bomb went off at 6.30 pm the next day. Seated on the floor of a relative's house, the immediate, mind-numbing shock seems to have given way to the slow but painful realization that her life partner is finally no more for Lakshmi. But she can't stop talking about the man whom she fell in love with when she was 18, the man who had to be reminded 'birthdays are meant for surprises, so surprise me', the man who, until a fortnight ago, gave her regular rides on his moped – a ten-year-old Hero Puch. 'A few days ago, I offered to buy him a car,' says the grieving mother of two. He promptly refused and replied, 'I won't be able to feel you close to me... a car's seating will leave too much space between us.' Srinivas's job brought the Raos to Bombay in 1975. He had left his home state of Karnataka for Jabalpur (MP) in 1966 after matriculation, for a Central Railway posting, then got married to Lakshmi, after which the transfer happened. 'We were both from families bound by tradition. On our own in a new city, we were like free birds. We never stopped flying,' recalls Lakshmi with a wistful smile. Yes, they were quite a couple; and age never came between them.

SWAPNIL OKE

When the UTI job offer came it was too late

He never really wanted to stay away from Mumbai. But the daily commutes were getting to him – he had only recently changed jobs to join DHL to avoid working the late-night shift. Now, to better his prospects, he had applied to UTI Bank, agreeing to a posting anywhere in the country. Ironically, when he did get the call to discuss the new job, it was too late. Swapnil Oke (27), like a typical Mumbaiite, never wanted to leave the city. And it was only recently that Swapnil grudgingly gave up his whole-hearted allegiance to Mumbai. 'He went for an interview with UTI bank after agreeing to work anywhere in the country,' says his father. 'Two days after the blasts, we got a call saying he had got the job.' Equally passionate about books and sports, Swapnil graduated from Royal College, Mira Road – he was in the college football team, says his younger brother Shreyas – and had already started working even as he pursued an M.Com (distance learning) from the Kalina campus of Mumbai University. 'I was confident that if he went for any exam – bank, competitive, or even an interview – he would be successful. He used to read anything and everything,' says his father. On Terrible Tuesday, Swapnil was last seen by a friend as he was boarding the train at Bandra station. 'Living in Mumbai and travelling by train, you know what time you leave home but never know when you will came back,' says his father Prakash. Or, indeed, if you will ever come back – and that's the grim new reality of Mumbai city that this devastated family is trying so courageously to cope with.

ASHOK VAGHELA

When his CA firm prospered, he bought a new apartment.

It's not the memory of the 13 years she spent with Ashok Vaghela (40), after she married him at 21, that gnaws at Yogita. It's what those years have left her with and what they've taken away. 'He was, in every sense, the head of this family. His was the last word – all decision-making was left to him. I was happy taking care of the home. I feel completely directionless now. Also, I am equally tired of the well-meaning advice everybody leaves me with,' she says. In the comfortable home they'd set up in Borivali's Rustomjee Complex, she's been particular to keep her young children, Kewal and Shraddha, busy with school and tuitions. A commerce graduate from Parle's Chinoy College, Ashok's success is something Yogita remembers he had laboured for right from the days of their courtship. 'His friendly nature would win everyone over, especially his clients,' she says. Besides his job, Ashok was also the treasurer of the building's Society. Though his extended work hours were the one complaint Yogita had against him, keeping alive his vision of the firm he set up is now a priority. For Yogita, the things that he did and said seem prophetic. 'He'd always rue that I don't think ahead. Today, looking through his financial papers, I see everything has been meticulously taken care of, as if he had prepared for any situation. That's so much like him. I still feel he's out there, working late as usual,' says Yogita who has been affected by severely disturbed sleep ever since his death. 'I miss talking to him. Shraddha, my daughter, was asking me the other day, "Ma, what kind of people do this?"'

Benny Joseph

A grocer from Kerala who made Mumbai his home

Benny Joseph (34) was a fighter; he took disappointment in his stride. When the armed forces turned him down in 1999 in New Delhi for having a 'defective heel' he did not let it get him down. He stayed on in the capital and started a 'Kerala Shop' selling banana chips, pickle and other coastal delights. Four years later, he was in Mumbai. At the time of his death, Benny's tiny enterprise had grown to two Kerala Shops, while he himself had found employment as a sales executive with Prime Enterprises in Charkop. 'I have lost my right-hand man,' boss and friend P.C. Sergent said when Benny succumbed to his injuries two weeks after the attack. His seven-year-old daughter clings to her grandmother. 'Beeba is too young to understand what's happened, but around 9 pm, the time her daddy would come home, she becomes restless,' says Benny's mother, Mariamma. Beeba was very attached to her father, a divorcee. They all wanted Benny to remarry but he wanted to wait till his sister Rincy settled down. 'He brought us to Mumbai and now he has left us,' says Mariamma taking out photographs of her tall, strapping son from her purse. Helping others was second nature to Benny, so the family had hoped he was doing just that when they couldn't find him. 'Even when he was a little schoolboy, he would help in the Onam festivities and other activities in school,' recollects his mother. As the eldest of three siblings, Benny was always the responsible one. At school he was the sporting kind. Back home, in Alappuzha, his many certificates and trophies are testimony to this.

SHASHIKANT BADEKAR

Constable and athlete

Little Abhishek and Aditi have not fully grasped what changed on Tuesday, July 11. It will hit them when they are moved out of the only home they know. For their father, Constable Shashikant Badekar (32) ended up a victim of the serial blasts, his body chanced upon by a fellow constable on duty at Bandra's Bhabha hospital that night. Now, in Police Lines, an unassuming colony atop a little hillock in Goregaon, the primary problem for the Badekars is that Shashikant did not own so much as an inch of land anywhere in the country and eviction from the home they've lived in for decades is imminent; a wretched circumstance for a family that has given five men to the police force. 'Height–body *inke jaisa tha*,' says brother Vijay, pointing to two men in the room, over six foot two, with booming voices and worry in their eyes. In March 1991, before he joined the force, Shashi ran from Mumbai to Satara to mark the second death anniversary of former chief minister Vasantdada Patil. He was the torchbearer, says a little plaque. The medals in the showcase are evidence of his sporting prowess. There are also laminated photographs of Shashi in impeccably pressed khakis being congratulated for 'good detection work' by former police commissioner M.N. Singh. 'Commissioner Saab shook hands with him,' says his father. 'That's how good my son was.' 'If the railways can give Jaishree a job, at least the children's education will be taken care of,' sobs Shashi's mother. Jaishree, Shashi's widow, with two children clamouring for her attention, looks up at the mention of a job. It's up to her now, after all.

SUALEH SHAIKH

Education was his mantra

Besides the travel agency which he ran in partnership, Sualeh Shaikh (42) owned two shops in the Asmita Anita Complex on Mira Road. And when his friend Kulwant Singh wanted to rent one of its annexes to start a coaching class, Shaikh agreed readily. Only, he refused to accept rent. 'If you educate children, then the rent is free,' he told him. That was Shaikh – 'Sualeh Bhai' to his friends – who knew him as a 'jolly good fellow' with a green thumb and a single-minded obsession with education. 'The children's education was all he cared about – "I do not know any English, but my children should become English *afsars*" – is what he always said,' recalls wife Ruksana, whom Shaikh brought to this city three years after their marriage, from Uttar Pradesh. 'He was the most jovial person to know... always cracking jokes,' says Shahabuddin Khan, Shaikh's best friend, who had to identify the body before it was sent to his hometown in UP for the last rites. His teenaged son Danish talks of how his father would sometimes 'do good things behind Mummy's back'. Like filling Haj forms for all his close relatives, for instance. 'He told me not to tell Mummy as she would fret about the cost. But he did fill the forms and explained to me that he could afford to do this as his own primary responsibilities in life were all in order,' says Danish, defending his large-hearted father. Ruksana gestures to her son to be quiet. 'Eighteen years of a life together...eighteen years of love...will fill up your newspaper... let a few things remain in our hearts,' she says, wiping her tears.

Joseph Robert Noronha

Banker from 9 to 5; teacher in the evening

Joseph Robert Noronha (56) was a banker, but his heart was in a classroom. 'Day after day for over 25 years, all through his first stint as chief manager with the Bank of Baroda and later as manager with Greater Mumbai Cooperative Bank, he would get home at 5.30 pm and by 6.30 pm he would be with his students in the night school,' says Celine Rodrigues of Joseph, or 'Joy', the youngest of her four siblings. 'Sometimes I would go to visit him on Sundays only to see him leave for the school again,' she says. 'Then Joy would tell me, "You are my sister, Celine, you will be always be here, no? I have only this much time for the children."' 'Joseph was a sincere, hard-working soul,' says his neighbour K.K. Pujari, who first introduced him, in 1977, to the students of the Kannada-medium Sree Saraswati Night High School, most of whom worked in the local Udupi hotel on Grant Road. 'Every evening he would teach maths and science to the children and work wonders in just three hours. He also taught them on holidays, Diwali and Christmas breaks.' Later, when he grew older and couldn't keep up the pace, he spent his evenings at home in Malad with his wife Nancy, reading or listening to music. Jim Reeves was a particular favourite. Celine, who retired as a head nurse from Bhatia hospital, was the one who identified her brother's badly mauled body at the Sion hospital mortuary after two days of endless searching. 'On Thursday morning, I knew I had to find Joy, no matter what,' says Celine. She finally identified his body by recognizing a scar left by an earlier bypass surgery.

Chetan Sharma

His wife survived the blast, but he didn't

They say home is where the heart is. But for Delhi boy Chetan Sharma (30), his heart was firmly where his mother was. However, when a Mumbai-based Forex firm offered him a better paying job, he resolved to ignore his heart for a while and secure a happy future for his family. His reasoning was sound: 'He wanted happiness for all of us. And money can buy some of that,' explains his mother Neelu. That day Chetan spoke to his mother around noon and around 5.15 pm, he called his wife Bhavna asking her to reach home early. In less than half an hour both were on different trains, bound for the same destination – their Borivali home. Bhavna survived the blasts at Khar which occurred in the compartment next to hers, but Chetan wasn't that lucky. He boarded his train from Churchgate. Either the Mahim or the Matunga blasts killed him, say relatives, who aren't sure. That night, at Chetan's home in Delhi, friends and relatives gathered around Neelu. She has seen death twice before at close quarters. First her eldest daughter and then her banker husband who expired suddenly. But Chetan's death is more than she can bear. 'I spent 22 years of my life with my husband. But with Chetan, I lived the longest. He was with me for 30 years,' she says. 'He lived to keep me happy.' Now that Chetan is gone, who will call her every day to ask after her? Who will send regular parcels of medicines from Mumbai? 'My son loved cricket, chicken and dancing. And he looked so handsome in whatever he wore, any shirt, any colour,' she says, a mother's pride shining through her tears.

KIRTIBHAI SHAH

He would hum Rafi tunes as he did his Gujarati crossword

'We were to shift to a new apartment in Bhayander a week after the blasts,' says his son. Now, mother Suryaben and son Deepesh are trying to come to terms with their tragedy. Kirtibhai Shah (65), her husband, his father, died on 7/11. Deepesh has another worry. His father was the main earning member of the house. So far he'd got by, by doing the odd job. Now, the onus is on him to search for something full-time. On Terrible Tuesday, Kirtibhai was returning from his office, a shipping company in Marine Lines. Being an elderly person, he was guaranteed a seat and he would sit happily, humming Rafi, engrossed in his crossword (he was able to crack 90 per cent of them) all through the one-and-a-half hour journey. Deepesh is not sure which blast killed him. 'It could have been the one at Borivali or Mira Road. Usually, Baba took the 5.19 Virar Fast at Marine Lines. But if you go by the blast timings, he should have been on the train at Mira Road. I really don't know.' Suryaben, who keeps herself busy in prayer, has resigned herself to living on at Nallasopara for some more time. 'He would often sing songs with his friends on the train,' recalls his friend Bhanushali. 'He loved music, especially the songs of Mohammad Rafi.' Kirtibhai, his friends all agree, belonged to a generation of simplicity. Radio, cricket and music defined his life. 'During the early eighties, when we were still to acquire a television, he would spend all his time listening to the radio,' recalls Deepesh. '*Abhi na jaao chhodkar, ke dil abhi bhara nahi...* was his favourite Rafi song.'

Abhijit Ahiwale

Usually rode his bike to work; that day he took the train

When a bomb exploded on board a public bus in their Mumbai suburb over two years ago, Abhijit Ahiwale had come home sombre. 'What do these people get by killing innocents?' he had asked. Whether it was the Ghatkopar bomb blast, Mumbai's serial blasts in 1993, or stories from Jammu & Kashmir, says Abhijit's father P.N. Ahiwale, he was always deeply touched by the pain of the victims, though, unlike younger brother Amogh, Abhijit never aggressively expressed his opinion on such matters; he reacted emotionally. 'He was an extremely sensitive person,' says his father. Abhijit died in the bomb explosion near Mahim station on July 11 – painfully unlucky for somebody who rode his motorbike to work every day, except on Terrible Tuesday. Deep in grief, the family is yet to come to terms with the loss and refuses to be photographed. 'Abhijit was so dependable that I always thought he'd get home safe,' says his mother Ratnamala who had sat up dry-eyed until seven in the morning, assuming he'd show up any time. An MBA from Gawade Institute at Mumbai Central, Abhijit was a devoted employee, leaving home sharp at 8.30 am every day, rushing off without his lunch-box if it was even a minute late. 'His mother would run behind him,' Ahiwale remembers. 'But he'd be gone.' Having turned 26 on July 4, Abhijit threw a grand bash for his friends that weekend. 'He kept asking me to stay back, ' says Amogh, who was returning to Hyderabad, after a long holiday. 'But I said I'll just return the next time the family meets together in Nashik.'

187 MUMBAI LIFE STORIES

Jitendra Maniklal Shah

A father devoted to his disabled son

As on every day, Jay Shah, 24-year-old son of Jitendra Maniklal Shah, had boarded the bus for his special school in Malad after his father left for office, but he returned to a tragedy he couldn't quite comprehend. 'Bring him home safely,' he told his sister Sonali, 14 years his elder, as she left for Sion hospital to look for their missing father. Eight hours later, when she returned, Jay reprimanded her: 'I asked you to bring him safe. Why have you brought him like this?' It was only when visitors and relatives started coming in to mourn the death of 62-year-old chief accountant at Synthetic and Art Silk Mills Association Ltd. (SASMA), that Jay understood. 'For the next couple of days, Jay cried so much that we had to sedate him. He was also down with fever,' says Sonali. 'He's learnt not to cry now.' Like his father, whom all of them remember as a man of few words and a kind heart, Jay has grown quiet. 'He was a true follower of Jainism. He believed in the principle of live and let live and faced adversities with courage,' says Sonali. So when Jay was born mentally challenged, Jitendra was shocked and upset, but only for a short while. 'He told me Jay was God's gift to us. We knew Jay would never be able to work, so he would assure us often that he would leave enough money for his lifetime,' says wife Madhu. 'He worried for him, but he never gave up.' For Sonali, her father's most precious legacy is his faith and courage. 'Though he never visited temples, he was God-fearing and kind. He passed on these values to us and wanted us to live by them.'

187 MUMBAI LIFE STORIES

Hariharan Iyer

Loved Mumbai and her trains

The 6.24 pm blast at Bandra station on 7/11 ended 76-year-old Hariharan Iyer's 46-year-old love affair with Mumbai's local trains. Since October 1960, the company secretary had been taking a morning train from his home in suburban Malad to his ad agency office in South Mumbai's Fort area, and another from Churchgate station back in the evening. 'He loved Mumbai's Western line trains. Even if he was being offered a lift to town he would refuse, saying he preferred the train,' says daughter-in-law Kaveri. 'On holidays, he would seek an excuse to visit the station.' That Tuesday, he was in the first class compartment of the Borivali-bound train. At the Dattaram Ad Agency, whose finance wing a young Iyer joined four-and-a-half decades ago as a young Chennai man who had just moved to the city, they are all stunned. His boss, a grieving Lalita Raman, points out that Iyer, 'a workaholic who did not believe in retirement', wasn't meant to have come to office on Tuesday at all. 'Since April, he had been working Mondays, Wednesdays and Fridays. The previous week's heavy rains meant he had stayed at home. So he came on Tuesday also, keen on finishing work on a particular file.' Mumbai's work ethic and frenetic energy mirrored Iyer's, and so he firmly rejected any suggestion of leaving the city for a quieter town. In his Fort area office, pointing to the next-door cabin that has been empty since July 11, Raman shakes her head and says, 'I believe the State even had intelligence about an impending attack but did not act. This is not the way a gentleman like Mr Iyer deserved to die.'

Jaiprakash Soans

All packed up, the family was moving to Bangalore

Until the ominous phone call, this was one of the happiest days in the life of Jennifer Soans. After a four-year stint in Mumbai, her family was shifting to Bangalore. From kitchen accessories to the wardrobes, everything was in cartons. She was only waiting for her husband, Jaiprakash Soans (51), to return from work for the last-minute packing to be done together. But Soans, a social worker for 30 years, never returned. Jennifer lost the boy she grew up with in their hometown of Udipi in Mangalore, the handsome batchmate who was her sweetheart through college and her husband of 25 years. Son Jovian, who had grown doubly close to his father over the last few months, since his mother was away in Udipi where her younger son Jocyln was studying, said, 'Dad would cook for me after returning from office. We'd watch movies. He never brought his work home with him.' Jovian misses his father every time he hears a hymn his dad would sing, or spots a book – Soans was a voracious reader with a large collection arranged meticulously in a little home library. Soans was project manager for the NGO Action Aid International for ten years. Having just been promoted as head of fund-raising, he was being posted to Bangalore. He always wanted to make a difference on the issues that drove him – urban poverty, problems of slum dwellers, street children. Apart from work, he enjoyed music and played the violin, the guitar and the mandolin. 'My heart is not filled with bitterness,' Jennifer says. She'll live like her husband always did: 'Not preaching Christianity, just living it.'

Shashikant R. Doshi

An accountant who juggled two jobs

He detested rush hour traffic but Shashikant Doshi's obsession with punctuality forced him to commute by train. As on every other working day, he wolfed down breakfast to ensure he made it to the train on time. 'He would breakfast at exactly 8.30 in the morning. I had to drop everything else and stand by,' recalls wife Meena. Terrible Tuesday began like any other day, but the Doshis will remember it as a night of a never-ending wait. Unlike on rain-hit 26/7 in 2005 – when the family waited for Shashikant (65) who was trapped inside a train for hours before he managed to reach home to Mahavirnagar in Kandivali the next day – this night's wait did not pay off. Shashikant was on the Borivali-bound Local and he died when one of its compartments blew up at Jogeshwari around 6.25 pm. His body was recovered from Cooper hospital by his son Bimal at 3.30 am. An accountant by profession, Shashikant juggled two jobs: one at a private office in Matunga for the better part of the week and the other at Jogeshwari's Darshan Electricals Industries on Wednesdays and Saturdays. 'He was a very gentle man and never asked for extra money,' says Chandrakant Shah, owner of Darshan Electricals. Though travelling wasn't one of his greatest passions, he'd always wanted to visit Mahabaleshwar. 'About two years ago, the whole family went there for a holiday and he paid for everything and even hired a boat exclusively for us,' recalls Meena. Over the last year Shashikant was finally thinking of easing up a bit, giving up one job and concentrating on his hobbies – gardening and chess.

187 MUMBAI LIFE STORIES

ARVIND AGARWAL

Chartered accountant who wanted to move out of Mumbai

Daughter Abhivyakti hasn't cried once since 7/11 robbed her of her father. As Anjana clings to memories of her seven-year-old marriage to Arvind, breaking down every now and then, she wonders how her small daughter can show such extraordinary fortitude. 'I don't know where my child learned this. "Mama, you should start your life afresh," she tells me. "You should wear lipstick like before. I will never miss Papa. You are now my Mama and Papa."' Arvind Agarwal (34) died while he was returning home from a hard day's work – he was a CA with Houghton and HardCastle – by train. His body was found in Sion hospital. On Terrible Tuesday, she was in the kitchen when she heard about the blasts. 'Immediately, my daughter made me sit down and gave me a glass of water. She told me, "Don't cry, Mama, Papa will come."' Though Arvind loved the two years he had spent at this job, he hated the daily commute. 'But my husband wanted to move out of Mumbai. He did not like travelling by train. Everyday he would hurt himself either on the hand, shoulder or leg because of the jostling inside the compartment,' says Anjana. Today, if Abhivyakti is remarkably stoic as she keeps herself busy with a noisy toy computer and a host of other electronic gizmos Arvind had bought her from Ballard Pier, it must be because of her deep love for her father. Anjana realizes this. 'He would give his life for his daughter. Once when she needed blood because of a serious leg injury, he didn't allow me to donate blood. He said, "I will give blood for my daughter,"' says Anjana.

Ashok Bapat

An easy-going, jovial theatre enthusiast

Ashok Bapat (60) was meant to retire from the National Textile Corporation (NTC) as General Manager in August 2003. But, NTC had tremendous use for a man who had been working since the mid-1990s on the loss-making PSU's turnaround plan of raising funds from the sale of its defunct land in Mumbai. So, Bapat took up NTC's offer of superannuation. Accustomed to working late evenings at the NTC headquarters at Ballard Estate, Bapat along with his colleague headed home much earlier than was usual for him on 7/11, after attending a meeting in Parel. Both died in the 6.25 pm train blast at Jogeshwari, two stops before Bapat was slated to alight. Three weeks on, at his flat in Goregaon, wife and college lecturer Anjali is still too shocked to speak. The couple of 35 years came to Mumbai in 1971 when Bapat joined government service as a civil engineer with the Public Works Department. He moved to NTC in 1981, and that is where he found his calling. Says son Avinash, 'The years running up to retirement were especially crucial since my father was very involved with the company's revival proposal and how the land in Mumbai could help raise money for the Company.' Easy-going and jovial, and a theatre enthusiast, Bapat was also on the board of two local education trusts, and delivered engineering lectures in his spare time at city architectural colleges. At NTC, they haven't yet hired his replacement. 'I haven't filled his post yet,' says NTC's managing director Ramchandra Pillai. 'And I don't think we can. Because Ashok is irreplaceable.'

Sandford de Sales

Hockey star and Elvis fan

Though he was six-two you could easily miss the normally reticent Sandford de Sales. But put him among friends, and the club-level hockey star would morph into the Elvis fan he was, sticking to a single glass of wine to ensure he was able to escort the girls home, yet becoming the life of the party. Sandford (40) died on Terrible Tuesday while returning home from his Fort office to Borivali's IC Colony. He leaves behind wife Janet, daughter Alisha and brothers, Claudius, Francisco, Romulus, and Savio. Sandford was from a family of sports people – father Tony de Sales was a reputed player for the Western Railway during the sixties and seventies. No wonder he took to hockey. 'Sandford was an exceptionally gifted player,' recalls Cladius. 'It was just bad luck that he never made the transformation into the big league.' But Sandford's life wasn't all about sport. He loved music. 'He preferred the oldies, Calypsos and hip-hop.' His prized belongings were gifts bestowed on him by those he loved, including his first music system from Romulus and his first mobile phone from Savio. But there was another reason for his universal appeal. Sandford was always ready to help anybody, at any time. A relative recalls how Sandford once landed at the doctor's with his backache aggravated despite medication. On being probed, he confessed he had helped a stranger whose bike had broken down, by pushing it along with one foot as he rode his own bike all the way till the service station. 'And yes, he had a great sense of humour,' smiles Claudius. 'People, especially the girls, loved his company.'

SOMNATH DAS

Proud of his recently-acquired first class train pass

For Somnath Das (37), a Bengali from Kolkata, the first class local train pass he held was his only luxury in Mumbai. While most of his colleagues at Normans Ross & Co travelled to office in their cars, he took the train. 'He would often tell us, "Even though I travel in trains, I belong to the elite class of Mumbai since I travel first class,"' recalls his brother-in-law Rajib Saha. On July 11, he ended up taking his last first class journey. He was on his way home from Churchgate to Kandivali by the 5.45 Local. The Mahim blast at 6.25 pm killed him. When the finance executive first landed in Mumbai in 1994, he was hoping to make ends meet so he could marry his college sweetheart, waiting for him back in Kolkata. It was a journey he undertook to the land of opportunity to save himself, from what he deemed a 'claustrophobic Bengal'. 'He was in a hurry to marry me,' says Mahua, his wife of ten years. So the then 24-year-old Calcutta University commerce graduate took up ad hoc jobs wherever he got one. 'He wanted to start earning. He knew he had to find a firm financial foothold before he could marry me,' she says wryly. The weekend before Terrible Tuesday, he had taken out their eight-year-old daughter Sheona for *Superman*. 'Every night, he spoke to her before going to bed. He spoke about values and their importance in life,' Mahua says. The one thread that ran through all he said to her was his belief that people needed to stay grounded in the country's 'glamorous commercial capital' by being rooted to the Gandhian ideal of 'simple living and high thinking'.

VISHWAS THORAT

Led a simple life, helping others to change theirs

Three years ago, when Navin Rauniyar was staring at a dark future as he did not have the resources to apply to a foreign university, he met Vishwas Thorat (43), and his life changed forever. For Vishwas lived his life by helping others. 'I don't know where I would have been without his support,' Rauniyar told us from Texas, where he is now pursuing a Ph.D in Molecular Biology and Immunology. 'Many people called up after the blasts telling me how my brother had helped them in their darkest hour,' says elder sister Chitra Pawar. Like Mahendra Kumar, who can't believe his friend is dead. 'The year was 1986 and my wife was pregnant. I was penniless and did not know what to do. Vishwas saw me sitting in a restaurant, sipping tea. When I told him of my plight he took out Rs 1500 and thrust it into my hand.' On 7/11, Vishwas was rushing early to his Kandivali home to cook a meal for his 79-year-old bedridden mother Nirmala when he died in the blast at Bandra. Vishwas lived a simple life. His one-bedroom flat in Vasant Utsav, Thakur village, Kandivali was spartan, but comfortable. 'He shifted there from Mulund six years ago as it was easier for him to commute to office using the Central Railway local trains. Also, his job required frequent trips to the airport,' says brother-in-law Surendra Pawar. Usually, Vishwas would be with colleagues when returning home by the 5.30 pm Local to Borivali. That day, he simply boarded the first train that was pulling out as he arrived at the station. His mother says, 'If only he had taken his regular train home that day.' *If only.*

Nandini Naik

In mourning for her sister, who'd died six months ago

'I think I am ready for Gadbad, let's go on Tuesday the 11th,' said Nandini (27) to Meena, a childhood friend, referring to the local ice-cream parlour that served a sinful confection of jelly, ice-cream and custard. Meena remembers the phone conversation vividly, more so because it was almost six months to the day that Nandini had lost her younger sister Rachna. A return to their ice-cream trysts meant Nandini was finally coming out of mourning. But life was playing games again. Nandini's body was found at Borivali station on 7/11. The Naiks – grappling with the loss of two daughters in the space of a few months – are trying to understand the inexplicable. 'She must have called Nandini,' says their father Ramesh Naik, pointing to Rachna's photograph on the wall. 'They were always together in everything they did.' For Ramesh, Nandini was the 'pride of the house'; the 'accounting whiz' to sister Rachna's 'homemaker'. The joke in the family was that if a guest asked for water Nandini would point to the kitchen, while Rachna would also force a plate of Maggi on the unsuspecting visitor. Ramesh describes Nandini as the 'daughter with a bouncing ponytail who always dressed pretty'. The first class commerce graduate was the first in their Goan-Konkani family to crunch numbers. But after February 24, when Rachna accidentally fell in the bathroom and died of a brain haemorrhage, Nandini withdrew into herself. Ramesh's abiding memory of his elder daughter will always be of the last time he saw her, on July 12. 'Her face was without a scar, beautiful as always.'

RAKESH RICHHARYA

When the trains struck twice

A terrible irony pervades the story of the Richharya family in Virar, 63 km north of Mumbai. Fifty-year-old Rakesh Richharya, an engineer with the Western Railway for 25 years, died when a bomb exploded in a Virar Fast on July 11. Six years ago, a gruesome railway accident left his teenaged son Amit with both legs amputated below the knee. Friends and relatives describe Rakesh as an affable, homely person, always soft-spoken and very religious. But Amit, now 23, remembers one extra-special gift his father had – that of inspiring him with the courage to live. In 2000, when his son lost both legs, it was Rakesh who helped his son pick up the pieces. 'He always reminded me that even losing both legs was not the end of my life and that I could still have a normal existence,' says Amit, a third year student of BSc (Information Technology). 'Most important, he never made me feel that I was handicapped.' What he remembers best of that period are the days when he was learning to walk all over again, this time with prosthetic limbs. Father Rakesh and mother Aarti would accompany Amit on his early morning walks in the vicinity of Paranjape Colony at Virar, egging him to take one step after another. Rakesh, a senior section engineer, was always an early riser, spending most of the early hours in a prayer alcove in their house in Virar. After Amit's accident, his battle for survival took precedence over prayer and Rakesh would be up as early as 4 am for walking practice. Says Amit, 'Whatever little I am able to do today is entirely due to him.'

SHARAD BHOBTE

A man of few words but a friend and guide to many

On any working day, Sharad Bhobte (51), a senior manager with Punjab National Bank, would be the first to reach office. He would stay till at least 6 pm. On Terrible Tuesday, however, he left early as he had to be back the next day at 7 am to fill in for his colleague and second-in-command, K.J. Laxman. Helping colleagues at work, and in matters more personal such as their children's education and securing home loans, was Bhobte's nature. So when news of his death in the explosion on board the Borivali Fast at Mahim at 6.30 pm reached Laxman, his friends were inconsolable. 'Sharad was supposed to handle my 7 am shift the next day. It was customary for him to inform me before he left office every day. How I wish I had stopped him,' says Laxman. The mood at PNB's head office at Fort has been gloomy ever since. For Sharad, the reticent workaholic and 'resident consultant', was liked by all. 'He took work so seriously that he didn't skip office even once. All his 12 casual leaves are lying unused,' says Laxman. At Sharad's modest two-bedroom apartment in Borivali, the family is still trying to come to terms with the tragedy. Friends and relatives have always known his wife Usha to be bubbly and talkative, but now she has nothing to say and stares out of the window for hours – as if praying for a miracle she knows will not happen. If his son describes his father as the 'eternal introvert', sister-in-law Meera talks of Sharad as a stickler for neatness. And if there's one thing Sharad was passionate about, it was picnics. 'He always initiated get-togethers,' says father-in-law Madhusudan Walke.

BHAIRAVNATH SALVI

Polished gold by day, dreamt of owning his own home at night

After a hard day of polishing other people's gold, two friends would sit late into the night, outside their cramped room in the BDD chawl in Lower Parel and dream that one day they'd save enough to buy a home. Nothing fancy, just a room would do. And come what may, they'd be neighbours. Sagar More and his friend Bhairavnath Salvi (22) made all their plans together. But after 7/11, More is faced with a reality he is finding hard to accept: he will not have Bhairavnath as a neighbour any more. And he wasn't even in one of those first class coaches in which the bombs went off – his Rs 5000-a-month salary wasn't meant to be frittered away on a first class pass. Bhairvnath's south-bound train had stopped at Matunga at 6.30 pm, the exact time that the bomb on the Virar train on the next track exploded. He died instantly as he happened to be on the footboard of a second class compartment, just opposite the north-bound train's first class coach. Bhairavnath left Harlikhurth in Kolhapur district and came to Mumbai when he was 16 with his most precious possession: a Class XII pass certificate. And when he got to share a 180 square foot room with 12 others at the chawl in Lower Parel, he knew he was on the right track. For his father did the same when he came to Mumbai and worked in a mill during the textile boom. 'Bhairav reached Mumbai on July 17, 2000 and we trained together at RB Jewellery in Andheri for six-seven months, learning how to polish gold and silver,' recalls Sagar. '*Kaam mein use bahut dilchaspi thi, khaali baithna use achcha nahi lagta tha*,' says Sagar of his friend.

VIKRANT KHANVILKAR

Passionate about microbiology and cooking

He was the son all parents want. Loved by his friends and professors at Wilson College, he was passionate about two things – microbiology and cooking. One would get him up at the crack of dawn to be in time for the 7 am practicals at college from faraway Virar, while the other would prompt him to occasionally prepare a meal for his parents. But Vikrant Khanvilkar (19) will always be remembered for his spirit: a never-say-die attitude that would at times provoke him to admonish his father if he mouthed – even if rarely – a negative thought or two. 'It was because of this that he was able to fight for 19 days even after being grievously injured on 7/11,' says Santosh, still unable to come to terms with the loss of his only child. On Terrible Tuesday, after talking to his friends, the Khanvilkars tracked Vikrant down to Karuna hospital in Borivali. Vikrant was injured at the base of his skull and in the lungs, necessitating a ventilator. 'We tried four or five times to take him off the ventilator but his lungs were very weak,' said Dr D.K. Bose, medical director of Karuna hospital, Borivali. His microbiology professor, Dr K. Aruna says, 'It is rare to find such an inquisitive student and bright mind. We had noticed it in him in the first year. He would have become a brilliant researcher or scientist.' For the Khanvilkars time has stopped since July 11. Mother Jai has been bedridden since, while father Santosh is trying hard to recover from the shock, without much success. 'That Sunday (July 9), he had cooked egg bhurji for us,' he says, suddenly overcome.

Namdeo Chintaman Bhagat

Worked for chawl-dwellers' dream of moving to a flat

Namdeo Chintaman Bhagat (59) had a dream that almost every Mumbaiite could relate to – that of having a flat of his own. For over two decades, he persevered to realize the dream for himself and hundreds of his neighbours in Chawl No 148, Gaekwadnagar, in Malad. Bhagat, who would have turned 60 in three days, was only a few months away from moving into a new 540-square foot flat when a blast at Mahim in the Borivali-bound Local abruptly ended it all. *'Bole the ab yehi mera kaam hoga,'* says wife Sindhu, remembering how Namdeo planned to follow up the redevelopment of the chawl after he retired as a section engineer with the electrical department of the railways by July-end. Zarina Sheikh, a social worker, narrates how, over the years, Namdeo tirelessly wrote to various government agencies to improve amenities in this huge, haphazard sprawl of ground-storey structures ever since he first moved here from Vadodara in 1982 with his wife and elder daughter Deepti, then a year old. What Sindhu and daughters Deepti and Smriti were excited about that day was Namdeo's 60th birthday on July 14. 'Papa was very fond of new clothes. So I offered to buy him a new shirt over breakfast that day,' remembers Deepti. 'He laughed and said we will all go shopping together in the evening.' As they had planned, Deepti left work early. She was on the overbridge at Santa Cruz station when she heard the sound of the first blast that took place between Khar and Santa Cruz. 'It sounded like a thunderbolt...' she recalls. 'We waited a long, long time before coming home,' says Sindhu.

Anish Baindoor

Tata Motors' manager, he was always smiling

Shobha Baindoor couldn't see her husband but she knows exactly what a broad grin would have lit his face when he told her on the phone on Tuesday, July 11, that he was getting off work before 6 pm. After all, that dazzling smile is what everybody remembers Anish Baindoor (31) by. 'He never left work before 8 pm,' says Vinaykumar Baindoor, Anish's father, a retired engineer. 'He was a complete workaholic.' In this household, work was worship. And Anish, a manager with Tata Motors, was talking to his Pune plant on his cell phone even as he boarded the ill-fated train from Churchgate. That's why the family's most prized possessions now are the countless certificates of merit earned by Anish for everything, from fund-raising for the blind, to competitive drawing, to outstanding achievement in the classroom. There, along with picture-perfect family photographs of a handsome Anish, is a special condolence letter. It's signed by Ratan Tata himself. Anish's colleagues can't believe he's gone. 'He had a very pleasant and energetic personality,' said S.G. Saksena, but it was Anish's smile that was most special. Saksena calls it a 'disarming' smile, and the family believes it smoothed the most piquant situations. Everybody, from the sweeper to the household help mentions it and, in a photograph of row upon row of perfectly dressed men attending Tata Motors' annual dealers' conference in Sun City, South Africa, one 1000-watt smile stands out. That day, his brother bought home pav for his favourite pav bhaji. 'The pav came. Only he never did,' his mother says.

Laxmichand Nanji Gala

A CA by profession and a social worker by choice

Laxmichand Nanji Gala (55) did not have it in him to say no to people. But on July 11 he did just that—refused any work that came his way at his own accountancy firm in Dadar, determined to leave early to catch a play with his wife. And though his favourite Kutchi play was to be staged at 8 pm at Prabodhan Thakre Hall, a stone's throw from their Borivali home, he couldn't make it. He took the 6.17 Local, the first class compartment of which exploded at 6.35 pm near Matunga. A CA by profession and a social worker by choice, Laximichand's was a Mumbai success story. From a young village boy who lost his farmer father when he was two years old, to a city-based proprietor of his own chartered accountancy firm, a life story like his personifies the reason that Mumbai holds a special place in the hearts of millions in our country. After his first wife died in 1985 he married Urmila in 1986, when his children, daughter Falguni and son Chirag, were still small and missing their mother. 'But he never let sorrow stay in the house,' Urmila recalls. At his Chhasara village home in Gujarat, Laxmichand was brought up by his mother, who worked in the fields by day and cooked their meals for them at night. Yet he managed to join Mumbai's prestigious N.M. College of Commerce and Economics. Laxmichand graduated with a first class to go on to become the first CA from his village. Even though he had been living in Mumbai for more than three decades, Laxmichand never forgot his roots. 'He visited his village once a month, just to help people in need,' says Urmila.

Suresh Chand Pandey

Life and death in the railways

Life is said to throw up some strange ironies, and the story of Suresh Chand Pandey (50) can corroborate this. As a village boy, he studied under the fuzzy lights of the railway station at Jigna in UP; 22 years of his professional life were spent with the Indian Railways; and on July 11 he was on an earlier-than-usual train when he died in the blast at Matunga. 'My grandmother said he was so fascinated by trains that while doing his schoolwork he even befriended the stationmaster and learnt the basics of the railway system from him,' says son Nalineesh, youngest of three, at their new home in Evershine City, Vasai where the family had moved barely a year ago. Suresh's last assignment was as GM with RITES Private Ltd, an autonomous railway body. Family and friends describe Suresh as hard-working, honest and simple. Suresh's simple moorings came from a life of hardship and struggle. Else how could this village boy from UP become, first an electrical engineer from Motilal Nehru Regional College, Allahabad, and then go on to do an M.Tech in Information Technology from BHU? A self-taught computer wizard, it was Suresh who opened up the world of computers to his sons. But ask the boys about the one characteristic they would always remember their father by, and their choice is unanimous: honesty. And they have many tales to share. When the family lived in official accommodation at Bhadwar Park in Colaba, Suresh, then a senior officer, adamantly refused official transport to go to work, maintaining firmly that it was a waste of government resources.

Trikamlal Pandya

Doting grandfather and father

July 11 was a special day for Trikamlal Pandya (72). It was his favourite granddaughter's birthday and Devanshi – excited as she was about stepping into her teens – went to her Dada's modest Goregaon flat at 6.30 am to meet him before heading to school. Else, she'd have had to wait till late evening, when he returned from his daily visit to the Mumbadevi temple. Devanshi took a wise decision; Trikamlal didn't come back that night. 'He was body number seven at Sion hospital. Fully clothed with chappals on. Had he not been in the morgue, we would have thought he was sleeping,' says daughter Usha. His belongings were inside a plastic bag: a rudraksha chain, a small case containing his telephone book, wallet-sized pictures of deities with shlokas, money, and a small plastic bag containing last year's rakhis. 'He would always carry the rakhis with him saying, *"Yeh meri behen ne bheji hai, yeh meri raksha karengi,"*' says Usha. For Trikamlal, Tuesday started like any other day, since 1993 when he'd retired after 30 years of service with LGD Associates, Colaba. For the deeply religious septuagenarian, the day began at 6 am watching the Sanskar channel on television and then sitting for a two-hour-long puja at home. After a light lunch, he would set out for the Mumbadevi Temple in Kalbadevi. 'This was the routine Papa followed for the last 13 years,' says Usha, who after her mother's death in 1993, gave up the idea of marriage and lived with her father. 'He brought us up like boys. He worked hard and ensured that all of us graduated, so that we could fend for ourselves,' she says.

SANJAY SHIRKE

UTI employee, meticulously organized, religious, pious

For 11 long days, Sanjay (35) was among the 644 injured – he had left his Churchgate office of UTI-IAS early to attend a Guru Purnima function later in the evening at Kandivali. In fact, moments before a bomb ripped through the first class compartment of the 5.57 Virar Local in Matunga, he had called elder sister Aruna to check if she wanted to accompany him. Both couldn't make it to the function. Sanjay was grievously hurt and had to be rushed to KEM hospital, while Aruna had to rush to Borivali to be with his wife, Apoorva. Sanjay passed away on July 22 – doctors said he died of toxicity from the chemicals in the explosives. Things were only beginning to fall in place for Sanjay, third of six siblings. A fortnight ago, he'd got his driving licence and had decided to buy a car if not by Ganeshotsav, then definitely by Diwali. And while he was battling for his life in hospital, the passport reached home. 'His brother-in-law works in the UK. He had called them for a trip and Sanjay was eager to go,' says Rajesh, his elder brother who is a software technician. 'He was a pious and religious person without any addictions,' says college friend Manoj Dalvi, who remembers him as a 'master administrator' for having planned and executed a memorable trip of friends and family to Darjeeling two years ago. Being organized was second nature to Sanjay. 'Each and every electricity bill he paid, his own salary slips, and every record was meticulously maintained by him in a file and also on the computer,' says Rajesh.

Surendra Ramachandran

A walking-talking encyclopaedia on cars

Like most young men his age, 22-year-old Surendra Ramachandran loved speed and itched to ride a bike. But mother Sushila never allowed it, fearing an accident. The railways, she trusted. Sadly, returning to his Borivali home from father Ramachandran Subaiyya's Wadi Bunder office – the son was familiarizing himself with his father's customs clearing and forwarding business – Surendra had taken the 5.50 pm Borivali Local. 'He was not even working with me yet, he would come on alternate days since his GNIIT classes were only thrice a week,' says the father. 'He had bought a first class pass that very day,' says Sushila, breaking down. After a week of travelling second class, 'uncomfortable and cramped', he had insisted on it. He was their 'encyclopaedia of cars and all sorts of gadgets'. In the apartment, the drawers and cupboards are still stuffed with his collection of cuttings from the motoring sections of newspapers, plus his vast stacks of motoring magazines. Often, say the Ramachandrans, those meeting their son for the first time would assume he was an automobile engineer, so impressive was his detailed knowledge of the subject. 'He was so passionate about cars that he knew even the technical details of various models,' says Sangeeta. Neighbours routinely consulted him when contemplating a new set of wheels. Even at their last family outing at the Inorbit Mall, Malad, on the Sunday before he was killed, the plan had been to buy miniature cars for a brand new display case in the simple living room.

Aejaz Sheikh

Doting father, who dressed his family in the best brands

Midnights were their special time. He would be back from a day of hard work, and she would be waiting for the doorbell to ring. Father and daughter would then chat animatedly about homework, school gossip and growing up. That is how ten-year-old Anam will perhaps remember her 'Abba jaan' Aejaz Sheikh (41). As for her brother, ten-month-old Affan, he is playing with a ball, oblivious to the tragedy. Father Moeen feels their link with the mainstream world outside has suddenly snapped. Be it a decision on the education of a youngster, a career option for his brothers-in-law, or investment matters for his sisters, it was Aejaz's word the family depended on. Brother-in-law Feroze Ahmed Sheikh recalls how easily Aejaz would mingle with the crowd. 'He always assimilated into his surroundings, never encouraged any differentiation.' Recalling granddaughter Anam's midnight trysts, Moeen Sheikh says, 'The father-daughter duo would have the entire household's sleeping schedule on hold. The two would race to the breakfast table each morning and continue their conversation, which would invariably centre around new clothes, toys and what her friends thought. On July 11, the 'suitable boy' – as his mother-in-law called Aejaz – died on a Virar-bound train after a bomb ripped through its first class coach in Borivali. 'Painting the walls and furniture was next on his to-do list,' wife Shagufta says of her 'handsome husband who loved wearing the best brands'. Today, she yearns for a whiff of the cologne that once lingered in the staircase long after he left for work each morning.

187 MUMBAI LIFE STORIES

Suresh Engineer

A railway man, he loved the movies and the songs of Mukesh

At work, Suresh Engineer (58) lived his name. A junior section engineer with the railways' electrical department, he left office early that day but skipped his routine visit to his mother. Instead, he had rushed home to find out how his daughter had fared in her job interview. But he never did find out. Engineer died in the train blast at Borivali on 7/11. Three days later, Amruta got a job as an accountant in a multinational jewellery firm in Andheri. 'He was very eager to know about my interview. We spoke at 2.30 that afternoon, but my interview was not over then. So he must have been rushing home. He was really keen that I get this job,' she says. Engineer – the eldest of seven siblings – started working early. He got his first offer while he was studying in Class IX. The job was in the railways and he jumped at it. A workaholic, Suresh would be on his toes always – even on Sundays. But the evenings were reserved for wife Nirmala. 'Every Sunday he would go out with her. That's the only day they could spend some time with each other. It would be a short trip together but it was exclusively their own,' recalls Amruta. Suresh was due for retirement next year. And he had already made plans for the years ahead – he was thinking of opening a small shop, either in Nallasopara or somewhere else in Mumbai, to keep himself occupied. His family will miss him for the father he was and the elder brother he had been, while his colleagues say they'll keep talking of the 'jolly good man who loved to eat chicken and mutton', for a long time.

187 MUMBAI LIFE STORIES

Kunal Shah

He gave his seat to a stranger; later she rushed him to hospital

On 7/11 Kunal (23) did something rarely done on Mumbai's suburban commutes. He gave his seat to a woman in a packed first class compartment. He was twenty minutes away from his Goregaon home station. At 6.24 pm, a blast ripped through the coach. He died in hospital. The lucky woman survived without a scratch. It was this woman who rushed a profusely bleeding Kunal to the nearby V.N. Desai hospital in Santa Cruz. Later, she even went back to the station, for Kunal had apparently requested her to look for his friend and colleague, Hetal Shah, who was in the ladies' coach. Kunal and Hetal had boarded the Borivali Local from Dadar but had taken different compartments. 'Kunal seems to have asked the woman to take care of Hetal and ensure she got home safely,' says cousin Ashish Shah. Family members have managed to piece together the details of that dreadful evening from various eyewitnesses. The elder of two brothers, Kunal was an MBA in marketing from Bharti Vidyapeeth, Pune. Despite being five years apart, the two were close. Football, discotheques, the gym, or weekend parties with friends, they loved having fun together. The last time the two went out was to see the World Cup soccer finals at the Inorbit Mall. Since the last three months, he was working with Magna Publications as an advertising executive. At Magna, they loved their young ad executive. So they dedicated the August issue of *Stardust* – the publication he was attached to – to his memory. 'His colleagues say, this is the first time it has been done for an employee,' says his mother proudly.

Satyavan Biradar

Preferred plays to going for films, social outings

At the Biradars' home, you feel sad, even depressed. But you are compelled to smile through your tears when you realize how much happiness Satyavan Biradar (52) brought to his family. To his children, son Nandkishore and daughter Kishori, he was everything. And even if his old-style marriage wasn't exactly to his wishes (wife Shakuntala saw him only after the ceremonies), the subtle romance he infused in it was touching. 'He never drank tea, but if I was watching a film on TV, he'd never fail to bring me a hot cup. You know, he's the one who taught me how to cook. I never managed to better him at it. Especially, the sheera he prepared. On weekends, when he'd try his hand at something in the kitchen, we'd bet on the outcome,' says Shakuntala. She was very much the village girl married to one who went off to the city and made it big. As officer-on-special duty at Mantralaya, Satyavan had stepped out of his village Tapshal, on the Maharashtra–Karnataka border, to become a deputy director in the planning department. And within the walls of their flat in Dudh Darya Apartments, each member found fulfilment. Kishori and Nandkishore did well in all mathematics examinations. 'He was an MSc in Statistics and supervised us well with our studies. He would insist that we spend time on quality reading. He last got me one of Jayant Narlikar's books and, for my brother, our President's autobiography,' says Kishori. 'When I think about the relationship some of my friends share with their fathers, I realize how much of a friend mine was to me,' says Nandkishore.

187 MUMBAI LIFE STORIES

ANIL SHAH

His daughter waited with a special anniversary gift

Anvi Shah was all prepared with a surprise for her father – an enlarged photograph of his wedding, 24 years ago. But Anil Shah (49) never got his surprise gift. On July 11, the diamond broker was returning home early, rushing to participate in a religious function, but his journey to Goregaon ended at Mahim at 6.26 pm. Just a few days before he died, the family of seven had laughed together while thumbing through some old photos – they'd all looked so different then. 'Suddenly, out of the blue, he'd decided to clean the cupboard where all the family photo albums were,' remembers Aruna, his 48-year-old widow. She didn't know it then, but the Shahs had been sharing one of their last happy minutes together. Their son Ronak had recently cleared his CET exams with a score of 81: 'He was very happy. Ronak was falling short by a few marks for admission into the best engineering colleges, but Anil was still very satisfied.' For Anil, all three children were a source of great happiness. Anvi's wedding had been fixed in Virginia. Though he'd ribbed her endlessly about this, he had made ambitious plans for their forthcoming trip to America. At KEM hospital's morgue, early on July 12, the mood was grim. The end was gory. The athletic build of one body and the brand of clothing on it matched Anil's but there was precious else to identify him by, as the face had been completely destroyed and little more than his socks and briefs were left on his person. A post-mortem confirmed the worst – there was no gall bladder. Anil's gall bladder had been removed in a surgery a few years back.

187 MUMBAI LIFE STORIES

ANANDNATH TIWARI

Railway auditor, hurrying home to help daughter with maths

Working for the railways, Anandnath Tiwari (40) knew all about trains. So to get back to his Nallasopara home from Mumbai Central everyday, he would take a mail train rather than a local. The Mail, he knew, was faster and stopped at Virar, which meant he would have to travel back only one station, thereby avoiding the rush hour crowd. 'The mail train was late. But despite his boss's insistence, he took the Local as he was in a hurry,' recalls wife Kiran at their modest residence to which the family has just returned after a three-week stay in Allahabad for the last rites. That Tuesday, a quiet, 12-year-old girl lost her father; a loving wife of 13 years, her husband; and the Western Railway an assistant audit officer. Daughter Kashika, who looks wiser than her years because of her spectacles, has just gone back to school. Rangoli – the name given to her by her father, as he thought she had brought colour into their lives – has been extremely subdued. 'She is like her father. She was closer to him than to me. She would sleep beside him, hugging him through the night,' recalls Kiran, adding, 'She has grown up a lot in the last one month.' Anandnath loved his daughter a lot, which says much about the man from a country known for its unabashed preference for the male child. 'We had decided we would have only one child. After Kashika was born, he had said he would give her the best of education. So much so that everyone with sons would say, "We would rather have a daughter like Rangoli,"' recounts Kiran.

S. Krishnan

Retired SBI employee, awaited the birth of his grandchild

Living at his elder daughter Prabha's house in Goregaon as his wife Lakshmi was away, Krishnan (60) used the opportunity to do what he loved doing – spoiling his grandkids, nine-year-old Akshay and five-year-old twins Abhishek and Ashwin. This September, the plan was to do the same at younger daughter Sandhya's Bangalore home as she was expecting. But on July 11 a ride home from work – post-retirement, he'd taken a job with the Arab and Bangladesh Bank– shattered that wish. Krishnan, a happy-go-lucky man who loved to live, was the kind of person you would like to sit beside on a long train journey. Always up-to-date with information about anything and everything, he relished a good conversation. 'We would talk a lot about astrology,' recalls Lakshmi. No wonder Krishnan was always welcomed by Prabha's in-laws. 'He was never my daughter-in-law's father, but more like my elder brother,' says Prabha's mother-in-law, also called Lakshmi. She and her husband have the same names as Prabha's parents. 'Everyone called him Babu and mother Thangan to distinguish the couples,' says Prabha. The children, however, had their own name for him. They will miss the funny songs 'Babutata' would make up for them. 'Babu could get along with anyone. He would himself become a kid with the children,' says Prabha. She will miss her sporting father, who was always game for anything – be it a Sunday trip to the neighbouring Hypercity Mall or taking the children to Great Escape, a water park. For Krishnan being 60 was not an issue; he was young at heart.

187 MUMBAI LIFE STORIES

Asim Kumar Bhajan

In Mumbai for 16 years, he'd just bought a flat in Kolkata

A fortnight before the July 11 blast took his life, foreign exchange dealer Asim Kumar Bhajan (45) had concluded a trip to his native Kolkata and zeroed in on the flat he wanted to purchase for life post-retirement. Six weeks on, his deeply distraught wife Kakoli says in halting Hindi, 'He had come to Bombay in 1990 after being offered a job by DSP since he saw a bright future here, but he was deeply attached to Kolkata where he had lived till he was 30.' She describes Asim's life's passions: travelling and music. 'He was just back from Kolkata in June, and had bought several albums of Rabindrasangeet. He also loved playing the tabla. In fact, that's how we got to know each other: I would sing at local competitions while he played the tabla.' Asim had not just finalized the flat in Kolkata, but had also spent the summer renovating his Kandivali flat. 'He looked into every detail of paint and lighting himself. He said it was long due.' Neighbour Seema Dasgupta recalls being invited by Asim to the newly done-up house. 'With our busy lives I never ended up going,' she rues. He was similarly enthusiastic when it came to organizing the Durga Puja in the colony, going from door to door for collections. Deeply religious, Asim spent an hour each morning in prayer. He was also very conscientious about his health, and religiously went for a monthly-check up. 'He often said, "If something happens to me, how will you and Aniruddha manage?"' recalls Kakoli. So he kept a close tab on his blood sugar and cholesterol levels. What a cruel irony that he died in a terrorist attack.

187 MUMBAI LIFE STORIES

NATHUMAL SABOO

Had beaten cancer, and resumed work the day before

Nathumal Saboo (64) was a fighter. Having completed three months of radiation therapy to treat a malignancy in his throat, he was now in remission. Armed with new hope from his doctors – 'The lump had reduced in size, it wasn't that threatening any more' – he rejoined work on July 10. But what cancer couldn't do, a train ride did, the next day at Mahim railway station. The family had been through a crisis four years ago when Nathumal's wife died of brain haemorrhage. But then the family had come together to support him. Sons Subhash and Santosh started living with him. A month after his father's death, Subhash just can't make himself go towards Mahim. 'It was only yesterday I had to pass Mahim station. All the memories of that night we went searching for him came back to me in a flash,' he says. Their modest home in Sundar Nagar in Malad has changed forever since that day. What was once a happy, cheerful set-up is filled with gloom and pent-up anger. 'I am not sure the culprits will ever be brought to book here. Look at the number of blasts that have taken place in Mumbai,' says Subhash, who lives there with his wife Rekha and younger brother Santosh. But Nathumal wasn't pessimistic about the system. He had been working in Congressman Murli Deora's office for over 30 years. And even the politics of the day couldn't change him. Perhaps it had something to do with the generation he belonged to. 'He had been working even when my grandfather was alive,' says Murli Deora's son, Milind. 'He was a trusted, loyal, diligent worker. Our entire office grieves for him.'

Sunil Birwadkar

All he wanted after the floods was to move out of the chawl

Sunil Birwadkar (40) was fed up of having to carry his shoes and socks in his hand as he waded through knee-deep water outside his chawl every morning when he set out for work. Finally, the deluge of 26/7 was reason enough for him to take the plunge and buy a small flat, to ensure that his family, of mother and wife, would be safe indoors. The three of them moved to their new flat in Parekh Nagar – he was particularly fond of the location as it was near his sister Mohini Mahadik's house – in July. On July 11, a blast in his train at Matunga station killed him. 'Every single piece of furniture in this house is new, except for the TV and fridge. He loved the fact that our lifestyle had changed for the better. Unfortunately, he wasn't able to enjoy it for too long,' says wife Supriya. Colleagues describe Sunil as a soft-spoken, if not shy, person. 'He would prefer being left alone,' says Amogh Moghe about the man who liaised with banks in matters relating to foreign exchange. 'He had a different nature and we accepted him the way he was.' Indeed, Sunil was a very private person. If he saw his office crowd get into a particular first class compartment, he would choose another coach in which to travel, recall his colleagues. Brother-in-law Mahadik agrees. 'He would come to work on time, and go home when he finished,' he says. 'But he was also extremely helpful and cooperative whenever we needed something,' adds Moghe. That was Sunil. A simple man, diligent and dutiful, who took care of his family and had little by way of demands. All he wished for, perhaps, was to be left alone.

Kantilal Gohil

BMC engineer, his daughter's wedding was on the cards

'He was very intelligent. It was on his own initiative that he pursued engineering,' says Tulsidas Gohil of his son, who was an executive engineer with the Brihanmumbai Municipal Corporation (BMC). 'He used to say he wanted to be a professional and not a businessman.' Nearly two months after his sudden death, his family at their Borivali (East) home is still trying to come to terms with the big void his absence has left. His young son Aditya misses his father and says he didn't mind so much when he occasionally scolded him for not studying. His younger daughter Shreya can't bring herself to talk of her impending wedding. And Kantilal's elder daughter, Shruti misses her father's gentle ribbing of her husband. But it is Kantilal's wife Saroj who has had to bear the trauma of losing a loving husband and a devoted family man the most. Three days before a train blast near Bandra killed him, Kantilal (56) took his family to shop for Shreya's wedding. 'It was a Saturday and we bought sarees and other stuff,' says Saroj. Kantilal was looking forward to the December wedding, says Shreya. 'December was always special to him. He married Saroj on December 14, 1980 and Shruti was married on the same date in 2004. Kantilal was looking forward to his younger daughter's wedding. He was about to be promoted to deputy chief engineer. But more than all this, with two years left to retirement, he had already made plans for his free time. 'He loved to travel and was keen on going on a holiday to Europe with all of us,' says Shreya. He could not. And the family is left asking: *Why?*

187 MUMBAI LIFE STORIES

Rajnikant Panchal

Introduced his grandson to the stock market

Once a week he would go to the Dadar market to shop for vegetables and fruit for the family. More than his contribution to the house, it was the 70-year-old's way of keeping himself busy. July 11 happened to be his marketing day. Rajnikant Panchal didn't come back home. Rajnikant wasn't a first class traveller. 'But he must have got himself a seat that was near the first class compartment where the blast occurred,' reasons his eldest grandson Dhaval, as he stares at his sandals, a gift from his grandfather. A commerce graduate from Surat, Rajnikant had come to Mumbai in search of a better life. When the textile factory in which he worked closed down, he turned to the share market. In fact, grandson Daval developed an interest in the share market watching his grandfather note down prices from the TV scrolls. Like all grandparents, Rajnikant would dote on his grandchildren. But he would never hesitate to reprimand them if their 'demands grew beyond their needs', citing his own experience of hard work in this city of dreams. The Panchal house is full of his things, many of them associated closely with him – his blue notebook, in which he kept his share records, his watch, and his pocket FM radio on the table beside his bed. 'He was very fond of movies. Sometimes, he would go off somewhere without telling us and we would find a ticket in his pocket the next day,' says his grandson. Rajnikant adored Amitabh Bachchan and Kishore Kumar. Rajnikant's wife died of an illness 18 months ago; now the family is steeped in tragedy once more.

187 MUMBAI LIFE STORIES

Sumant De

Was looking forward to finally marrying his girlfriend

On July 11, instead of going to the Andheri office of the jewellery manufacturer Nakshatra, Sumant (23) headed to South Mumbai's traditional diamond market, Zhaveri Bazaar, to hand in some of his designs. 'He left my shop at 5.30 pm, refusing tea as he had to go to Bhayander to meet another customer,' recalls goldsmith Minto Ghosh. He took the train. A blast in the first class compartment at Mahim station at 6.26 killed him. At his Nallasopara residence, which doubles as a jewellery design workshop, family members and colleagues give more poignant details. Sumant's first class pass was just 11 days old, bought to escape the rush hour crush of the second class compartment. And this summer, when his parents visited Mumbai, Sumant had finally won their consent to legitimize his long-standing relationship with his girlfriend in Kolkata, Oindrila. She was the last person Sumant spoke to, minutes before starting what would be his final train ride. At the Nakshatra office, colleague Gautam Mukherjee remembers him as a dear friend. 'Sumant liked living life king-size. Whether it was a cell phone or dining out, he liked the good things in life.' 'He was working hard here, with an eye to going back to Kolkata and working on his own jewellery design business,' says sister Chaitali. 'He had even bought some land in our native village, where he was going to build a house.' Chaitali's abiding memory of her elder brother is that of a gregarious and large-hearted person who loved giving gifts and taking friends out. 'Dada loved people,' she says.

MAVJI PATEL

A diamond broker who loved to party

Commuting on the Western line between his Goregaon home and Charni Road office six days a week for the last 20 years, Mavji Patel (43) had a peculiar habit. He would never take a seat, even though it was a 40-minute ride across 15 stations in a packed compartment. He preferred standing in the train's passageway and feeling the breeze on his face. July 11 was no different. He was among those who died on the spot when a bomb ripped through the compartment at 6:26 pm at Mahim station. Patel, a diamond broker, was heading home earlier than usual for Guru Purnima as the family had planned to seek the blessings of their spiritual leader Guruji Wagji. Instead the family ended up going to Sion hospital. Mavji's last rites were performed in his hometown of Palampur, where the family had recently spent one of its most enjoyable holidays, in May, for a cousin's wedding. 'Papa danced so much at the wedding. I had never seen him like that,' says school-going son Gaurav. Yes, Mavjibhai loved to dance, says wife Ramila, recalling the numerous dandiya parties they had enjoyed together. And like the children, she will sorely miss their New Year celebrations. 'Every year we would go to parties organized by the Bhaidas Club, where we are members.' But there were some things Mavji disliked. Says Gaurav, 'He wouldn't let me sit next to him on the dining table if I was eating onions.' Like many fathers, Mavji was also passionately possessive about the TV remote. '*Kisike haath mein remote nahi aane dete the,*' his wife says. It was his way of unwinding after work.

Manish Divekar

Doing a course in stock-trading; had just taken his final exam

When toddler Aryan, wanders in from next door looking for 'kaka Manish', no one knows what to say. 'Manish kaka has gone on an aeroplane to a far-off place. He will not be coming back.' That's the best Manish's father, 64-year-old Mohan Divekar, and mother Madhavi can do. For the last two months they have been saying this to little Aryan, who somehow doesn't seem convinced. Manish (24), the Divekars' only child, worked as a salesman at a large shopping centre in Dadar. That day, he was coming home to Ramlochan chawl in Jogeshwari and was on the Borivali Local. The 6.25 pm blast on the train at Khar station killed him. Two months after Terrible Tuesday, if the Divekars are still struggling to come to terms with their loss, the chawl in Jogeshwari's Bandrekarwadi hasn't recovered either. For Manish had always been at the centre of all community activities. Be it a picnic, a sports meet, or a puja, he was always there, leading from the front. 'He realized that often the boys in the chawl did nothing but hang out in the street,' recalls friend Rakesh Mane. 'He wanted to do something constructive.' Study and work kept him away from home for long hours. So, finally, his parents persuaded him to quit his present job and start visiting the markets to make a career for himself there. On July 10, Manish quit his salesman's job and brought home his last salary. The next day, he had gone to the Institute for a final test. He appeared for it and took the Borivali train to come back home. He died on the way. Mother Madhavi says simply, 'He was a good boy.'

Pinaki Mukhopadhyay

SCI engineer; had planned a holiday in Tibet

Pinaki Mukhopadhyay (53) arrived in Mumbai in 1984, posted in the city by his PSU employer, the Shipping Corporation of India (SCI). On July 11 he was taking his regular train back from Churchgate to his home in suburban Kandivali, trying to reach in time to accompany his wife Kalyani to visit their local mall. 'My last conversation with him was at 4.30 pm, asking him to leave office as soon as he could, and try to accompany me to shop at D-Mart in the evening,' says his wife of 19 years. The housewife, in her mid-40s, recalls his last day, which began like any other: dropping his school-going daughters Prerna (15) and Dwitiya (10) off at the bus-stop, reading the newspaper at the breakfast table, and heading off – 'surprisingly grudgingly', she recalls – to take the local train to his office in South Mumbai's business district of Nariman Point. Pinaki had asked to be transferred to Kolkata in 2000, but soon moved back to Mumbai as his children missed life here. Kalyani recalls the dreams Pinaki had of making both his daughters doctors: 'Prerna is more like Pinaki, quiet and studious. Pinaki was very keen that she should study medicine and she will try for that. But Prerna also loves gadgets, and could teach her father a few things. She is keen on studying engineering like her father.' A travel buff, Pinaki loved visiting new places, and treated his family to two or three vacations every year. The Mukhopadhyays' last trip was to Sikkim, and that trip had spurred a desire to visit other places. Kalyani says wistfully, 'Tibet was where Pinaki said our next family holiday would be...'

SOJIRAM MODULAL

A railway engineer, came from Ajmer in 1979

For 17-year-old Akash, his father's shoes are his most prized possession. Preparing for his higher secondary examinations these days, he wears them regularly as a reminder of the great responsibility that is now on him: to take care of the family after the death of his father, Sojiram Modulal. A railway engineer, Sojiram's death has left his small family in a quandary. Wife Shradha says she doesn't even have the luxury to mourn. 'His father was very keen on him pursuing engineering, but now I have no choice but to push Akash for a railway job,' she says. Uneasily poised on a sofa in their two-room Nallasopara home, Shradha can only hope that Akash gets the promised job. On July 11, Sojiram was on his way home from Mumbai Central when a blast at Matunga killed him. Later, when the police came home to return his belongings, the only thing the family wanted to find in the packet wasn't there. It was his treasured watch, a timepiece he had inherited from his father. 'Akash searched the packet, but couldn't find it. He used to joke, "After Dad, I will use the watch,"' recalls Shradha. Sojiram, who started off as a teacher from Ajmer, moved to Mumbai in 1979 after he got a job with the railways. Later, he became a stationmaster and remained one for ten years. He continued to work his way up, ultimately becoming a CTNL engineer at Bombay Central Station. He was known as a family man. Like any father, he loved to share jokes and have long conversations with the children at the dinner table. Daughter Ankita was his 'reporter' and fed him all the news of the house.

YOGESH FUTANE

Had recently lost his infant son to malaria

For Shweta Futane, 19, who lost her two-month-old son Mayank to malaria in May, and her husband to the train blasts, life has been harsh. Yogesh (26), her caring, hard-working, and ambitious husband of two years, had finished work to board the 5:48 pm Borivali Local, eager to get home and put in a couple of hours of study. His MBA exams were scheduled for July 24. He was nervous, but satisfied about his progress. 'The only world he knew was his books. He would study in the nearby library for hours,' says mother Vijya about Yogesh, who was working as an office boy at the Shangrila India Estate but was eager to improve his prospects. The first step to that was an MBA and he was pursuing the degree by correspondence from Pune University. Hence his long hours away from home – first at work and then at the library. Yogesh kept mostly to himself, as he was busy chasing his MBA dream. He felt he was getting there and would often indulge himself by imagining the things he would do once he got that job. 'In June he bought himself a camera cell phone,' recalls Vijya. 'He was so happy, it was infectious.' Vijya says Yogesh even fulfilled her long-cherished wish of a pilgrimage to Tirupati in December last year, while Shweta regrets her decision of not accompanying them on that trip. 'I was two months pregnant then and didn't want to travel, although I knew Yogesh had planned the trip meticulously. He emptied his savings and used up the Diwali bonus,' sighs Shweta. 'We were just getting to knowing each other after two years of marriage,' she says in a small voice. 'Now I am all alone.'

PRASHANT SAWANT

Took the same train as his wife every day, except that day

For one-and-a-half years, Prashant Sawant (39) and wife Sangeeta had been working in Gitanjali Exports, a diamond firm on Charni Road. So they commuted together by train from their Goregaon home every day. But on July 11, Prashant finished early. He took the 5.59 Local at Charni Road and was killed in one of the blasts. The family does not know which one. All they know is that they are fortunate Sangeeta finished work at the usual time and escaped the carnage. Prashant dropped out of college while still an undergraduate and worked as a clerk in the godown department of Crown Mill for 16 years. He took voluntary retirement from that job in 2002 and had since been with the diamond export house. Luckily for the Sawant family, the small staff flat in which they had been living since 1967 – 'since bhai's birth,' says younger brother Rakesh – was transferred to them on ownership basis. And soon, Sangeeta, who was already working for the diamond export firm by then, helped her husband get a job there. Rakesh remembers the frantic calls he made on their cell phones on that Tuesday. Prashant's phone kept ringing and there was no reply. 'Around 7 pm, I finally got through to Bhabhi at Mahim station. His friend Amit, she told me, was at Lower Parel. Strangely, all three of them had gone their separate ways that day,' recalls Rakesh. These days, sometimes, when the yearning to catch a glimpse of him is too hard to bear, Amit plays the CD of his brother Jayesh's February wedding: 'Only to look at Prashant dancing and having a good time,' he says. 'Only to see him happy and alive.'

RUPESH RAHUL KAMBLE

Planned to study in the US

'Don't be afraid, I will earn much more than what you have spent on my studies. A job in the US as a software engineer isn't far away…' Rahul Kamble can almost hear his son, Rupesh Kamble (19), tell him this even today. For Rupesh, a bright second-year student of computer engineering, this was the only dream he nurtured. His life revolved around books, tuitions and discussing the future with his parents. Until it all ended summarily on July 11 on a train. One visit to the flat and it's clear Rupesh's only interest was studies: the house is stacked with books. A computer, gifted to him by his father on his 16th birthday, stands in one corner. Father Rahul is far removed from the world of books and computers, but he proudly points to them and says: 'You know, he came 19th in the Maharashtra Common Entrance Test. My son even cleared the All India Engineering Entrance Exam.' But mother Rupal would rather talk about her son's personality: 'He was very quiet, but intense inside. He hardly had friends. He was a home-bird. Since he hardly spoke, I had to guess what was going on in his mind from his actions,' she says, gazing at his picture atop the table. 'He would wear a simple shirt and jeans. Never complained about food or anything. At times, I would make pau-bhaji or idli sambhar – his favourite – knowing he would never ask.' Ratna, his sister who's a science student at Matunga's Ruparel College, says she has lost her best friend. 'Rushing to tuitions together, doing our homework together and eating together. I feel so lost without him...'

NARESH JIVRAJBHAI SALGIYA

Stockbroker who wanted his son to be a pilot

'Where are you? Are you coming?' That was Naresh's last SMS to his brother-in-law before boarding the Virar Fast on July 11, inquiring if he would make it to the Guru Purnima function at the Bhuleshwar Swami Narayan temple later in the evening. Forty-five minutes later, Naresh (32) was dead. The family found his body at Bhagwati hospital late at night. 'Naresh would never travel that late in the evening. He would avoid rush hour,' says younger brother Paresh, a broker in the city's diamond market. Usually, he would head for home in suburban Mira Road by 4 pm. 'Since he was religious, he left late that day keeping in mind the Guru Purnima function.' Both brothers came to Mumbai ten years ago from Bhavnagar to make a better life for themselves and their families. Naresh got into stocks, while Paresh chose diamonds. Slowly but steadily, they made it good. Work on their 'new and bigger flat' was under way – as both wanted their families to stay together and also have their parents come and stay with them. The Grihapravesh was slated for Janmashtami. A chemistry graduate from Bhavnagar, Naresh had specific plans for his little son Sahaj and would often buy him toy planes. 'Yes, he wanted Sahaj to grow up thinking he should be a pilot. He is doing that now. When we ask him about his future, he talks of becoming a pilot,' says Paresh. Well-built and athletic, Naresh used to play volleyball and shot-put as a child but did not follow a rigorous physical regimen. Realizing the need to stay fit, he'd joined a local gym only a week before he died.

LOTAN BEDISKAR

A prolific reader with a vast book collection

On July 16, the first Sunday after Terrible Tuesday, Vishwanath Lande asked his wife to prepare fish curry and chapatis. He then took a generous helping of the meal to the terrace and fed it to the crows and recited a short prayer ending with, 'may Lotan Bediskar's soul rest in peace'. Bediskar (47), Lande's boss at the Law & Judiciary Department in Mantralaya, often asked him to get him home-cooked fish, as non-vegetarian food wasn't cooked in his own home. On July 11, Bediskar left work around 5.30 pm, half an hour after making his request for fish curry to Lande, and died in the blast on the 5.58 pm Borivali Local. As a section officer, Bediskar's work at the Mantralaya kept him away from home for long hours. But the little time he managed to get was spent in the happy company of his grown-up son Dhiraj and daughter Amrita. On Sunday, two days before he died, Bediskar had gone for a routine medical check-up. 'On Tuesday, I got his test reports from the lab and called him up at his office around 3.30 pm to tell him all his tests were normal,' says his wife Sandhya. That day, since he had hinted he would be home early, Sandhya was expecting him by seven. But by midnight there was no trace of him. And when all their calls to him went unanswered the family stepped out in search of him. Dhiraj identified his father's body at Cooper hospital the next morning. When the police handed over Bediskar's body, they also gave back some of his belongings, among them was a watch that had survived the blast without a scratch. Sadly, the man who wore it was not so lucky.

SANAT MANUBHAI BADHEKA.

Tax consultant and secret philanthropist

The Badhekas are only now beginning to discover the reach of 47-year-old Sanat Manubhai Badheka's philanthropy, through neighbours, friends, and sundry youngsters, all of whom showed up at their Kandivali (West) home to offer condolences after his untimely death on Terrible Tuesday. 'I was surprised to see students of different colleges attend the funeral until I discovered that my husband used to pay their fees. All of them visited us to express grief at his death,' says his widow Bhavna. 'An old man came to me and told us his cataract operation was funded by him. In 50 years of my life, my husband gave me the happiness of 100 years,' she says, crying. 'On every birthday he would gift me gold. There was never a dull weekend. He treated his two daughters like princesses. '*Seth to raja tha,*' recalls security-man Sushil Singh. 'Recently, he ordered mangoes for all the guards. I love mangoes but can't afford them. I enjoyed them because of him. He gave us food and shelter during the Mumbai deluge.' For his daughter Puja, studying MSc at Thakur College, Sanat was a fun-loving father. 'He never scolded me for coming late on New Year's eve. His only condition was that I inform him.' Though he wasn't particularly fond of trekking, Sanat would often take Puja and her younger sister, Purvi, for a holiday to Matheran. After losing her father, Puja finds it difficult to even touch the cupboard that contains his vast CD collection. 'When I pick one up...I feel so empty... my head starts to spin.... the tears don't stop...' says Puja, pointing brokenly at the closed cupboard.

Ramesh S. Kumavat

Garment factory owner; had bought his new flat on a loan

'Papa ko train walon ne maar daala.' That's how nine-year-old Bhoomi, Ramesh's elder daughter, tries to explain the sudden death of her father. Her brother Vrushank, a year younger, seems to have taken it better. With two young children, a home loan and an uncertain future, Shweta hasn't really had time to mourn the death of her husband on July 11. Ramesh Kumavat (32), who ran a garment factory with a friend, was returning home particularly early that day, as he had to drop his parents at Borivali station; they had come visiting from their hometown of Phalna in Rajasthan. Looking back, Shweta remembers the uneasy feeling she had that day. 'I learnt of the blasts from a relative. I knew Ramesh was coming early that day and I remember feeling that something bad was going to happen,' she says. 'Our financial situation is crippling,' she admits. 'There is no support from my in-laws. I am desperately trying to convince them (in-laws) to permit me to accept a job.' Shweta remembers the day they moved in to their flat two years ago. 'It was the happiest day of our lives. But now, I haven't been able to pay the instalments since July,' she says, for the first time unable to hold back the tears. 'I have to bring up two children. How will I manage? Ramesh came to Mumbai when he was just 14 – he wasn't keen on studies and so his father asked had him to move on and look for ways to earn a livelihood. Five years ago, Ramesh and a friend started a garment company in partnership, specializing in ladies' wear. But now there is nothing left.'

JAGANNATHAN N. GUNDAPPA

A simple railwayman, his austerity was limited to himself

There is a sense of calm in the Gundappa residence, a single-bedroom flat on the busy Ambadi Road in Vasai. It is a quiet evening, and the family of Jagannathan N. Gundappa (52), a Western Railway employee, who died in the Matunga blast, is engaged in its daily chores. Padma, Gundappa's wife of 20 years, has just finished preparing dinner, son Raghavendra has two friends over, and daughter Monica is practising some geometry problems from her standard X textbook. 'Daddy would have wanted to watch *Saibaba* or that other serial on Ganpati if he were here, and tomorrow being Friday, he would have fasted to worship Goddess Santoshi,' says Raghavendra. 'Sometimes, I would tease Daddy about his simple ways, how he had been wearing the same shirts for years or how he always ate without a spoon. But he would just laugh it off. These things never mattered to him, he was so spiritual,' he says. But Gundappa's austere ways were limited to himself, insists Padma: 'He doted on Monica and for her happiness he would do anything, whether it was buying her expensive dolls or other gifts or helping her wriggle out of trouble if she had been mischievous,' she says with a smile. Gundappa had come to Mumbai in the seventies after completing his matriculation from a school in Mallasnagar village of Tumkur district. He worked in a garage first, and then in a bank, before joining the Western Railway as a clerk. Studying on his own, he took various examinations conducted by the railways. This May, he'd been made Officer Superintendent II in the engineering department.

NANDABALLABH DHONDIYAL

He never shied from helping friends and relatives

Much time has passed since Nandaballabh Dhondiyal (43) took the 5:57 Virar Fast instead of his usual 6:11 Fast and was killed in an explosion. But Khimanand can't stop asking why his father left early that day. 'I was at my friend's place while mother and Hemlata were home. No cell phones were working, so we could not contact Dad,' he says. The Dhondiyal home at Virar has been engulfed in silence since. His widow, Anandidevi, hasn't been eating properly. 'She has always been a poor eater but Dad's death has taken a toll on her mind and body. The doctor says she must eat properly for the medicines to work,' says Khimanand, 'but she doesn't.' The only time Anandidevi speaks is when she tells both Khimanand and Hemlata to 'study hard'. The teenaged girl misses her father so much that she has not been able to sleep properly. 'I just keep thinking of him. Everything I do reminds me of my father.' Nandaballabh had been working with the Western Railway as a senior clerk for 21 years. Two years after his marriage, the couple moved to Mumbai from Almora in Uttaranchal. Anandidevi describes her husband as a man of few words who never shied away from helping friends and relatives. But now the family has financial worries. With no earning member, it is becoming increasingly difficult to run the household. Most of the compensation money and Nandaballabh's Provident Fund has been used to repay the house loan. Even so, Khimanand has turned down a job offer from the railways. 'I'd rather complete my education and get a job that would make my father proud of me,' he says.

DEVESH SINGH

A collector and artist who enjoyed making pebble sculptures

Studying science at Bhavan's College in Charni Road meant a two-hour daily commute from his home in Virar, but Devesh Singh (18) didn't mind. At times, when friends would coax him to bunk a class or two, he would flatly refuse, telling them he didn't suffer for two hours every day to miss classes. 'Guddu (his pet name) got 68 per cent in SSC. He couldn't make the grade to study science in a suitable college in Virar so he took admission at Bhavan's even though it was a two-hour commute,' says mother Ritadevi. For the Singh household, two generations living together as a joint family, it has been a disturbing two months. Yet, a fascinating facet of Devesh that they are only now discovering is helping them take courage. Devesh was a collector. He had stored all that he cherished in a locker, which they now have access to. 'He used to keep his things in a locker and we never breached his privacy,' says Ritadevi. 'After his death we opened the locker and discovered a treasure trove.' Kept neatly inside were colours which he had got as gifts when he was in standard I, old toys, gift wrappers, coins and dozens of colourful rakhis, each with a tag bearing a serial number and the name of the sister who presented it to him. 'I realize now that whatever he cherished he never disposed off,' says Ritadevi. Devesh was creative too. His paintings, drawings and sculptures were part of his collection. 'Whenever he did something, he showed it to me. Among his favourites were sculptures he made by sticking together pebbles found on the seashore,' recalls Ritadevi as she organizes his works on a table.

Manohar Raut

Bank cashier, loved meeting people and making new friends

When Manasi got admission to a physiotherapy course in Mangalore a year ago, her parents decided to visit her as often as they could. The last time Manohar (54) and his wife Meena met her was on July 8. 'I made a huge fuss when both left the next day,' she recalls. 'I cried at the bus stand and told them to stay on. If only I had managed to convince them.' Two days later, on July 11, her father Manohar died in the Matunga station blast. Manohar started his professional career as a cashier in Sion hospital. But for the last 20 years, he was with the United Bank of India and was posted at the Fort branch as head cashier. That day, before he got into the Virar train at Churchgate, he met a relative, Anita Raut, who got into the women's compartment of the same train. She was the last to see him. Manohar had always wanted Manasi to become a doctor. 'When I got through, my mother was against the idea of me living so far away in Mangalore. But my father convinced her,' she says, recalling how they would visit her almost every three months. A trustee with a local Vasai social organization, Samaj Maha Mandal, Manohar had his own retirement plans. 'He was always a Vasai boy, having lived in a small village there. After retirement, we had plans of buying a house and moving back there,' says Meena. Through out the last two months, Manasi has been telling herself not to grieve for a man who spread so much joy. 'I feel he lived his life to the fullest. Pointing to me, he would always say, "After retirement we will relax... You will have to work."' Manasi would have liked that.

Suresh Shenpadu Pawar

A stern policeman but a soft father

Suresh Shenpadu Pawar (40) was a no-nonsense policeman, a committed worker, and a man of few words. It took long for even those close to him to not mistake his brusque manner for harshness. 'I would pester him with small talk when he would return from office,' says wife Suneeta, sitting in their small one-room rented apartment in Borivali.' But I never dared to call him when he was at work,' she says. The mother of two wears a forlorn look and her young frame appears bent under the weight of the responsibilities Suresh's sudden departure has left her to face alone. But her face lights up as she traces the journey of over a decade. 'I was 18 and had just passed standard XI when we got married. He taught physics at Kusumba High School; I found him intimidating,' she says of the initial years they spent in Dhule district. She breaks into a smile remembering the changes that living away from a joint family, after Suresh cleared the Maharashtra State Service exam, brought. They moved to Nashik with their son Digvijay, and later Suresh joined the state police service as a sub-inspector at the Borivali Police Station in 1996. The tough, conscientious policeman would soften his stance with children – his nieces and nephews who often stayed with him, and his sons Digvijay (12) and Prajanya (ten). For Prajanya, the best days were those that ended with huge helpings of the noodles that Pawar would sometimes buy him from a Chinese eatery on his way home. 'Daddy would scold me for not having daal-sabzi but I would stay awake, because I knew he would get me noodles anyway,' he says.

JITENDRA GANDHI

Grandfather, fascinated with his newly-acquired camera phone

On the night of July 11 Mitul looked for father Jitendra (60) in every possible place. Forty-eight hours later, he went to the police who showed him CDs of the blast victims. When he reached Cooper hospital, Mitul was told that his father's body had already been claimed by someone else. Even months later, that one statement still makes him shudder. Born in the small Gujarat town of Una, Jitendra completed his education living in a hostel as his parents died when he was only five. He moved to Mumbai in 1965 and tried to earn a livelihood – his first job was at Murji Jhetha textile market. Taking up a friend's suggestion, he later began supplying stationery to the income-tax department. It worked: for the last 15 years, he had been doing just that. Mitul says his father was self-made. 'He was a workaholic. Whatever little he achieved in life, he did by virtue of his hard work.' His wife Praveenaben agrees, but won't say much. She misses him, and his love for pooranpoli – on Terrible Tuesday, he had specially asked for some before leaving for Ayakar Bhavan, never to return again. But the memory Praveenaben cherishes most is of the evening tea they shared together on a swing. Jitendra loved that swing. Mitul also recalls how Jitendra had developed a fascination for a camera phone he'd bought on the 8th of July; he'd owned it for only two days. He remembers his father's selfless attitude, how he would never spend money on himself, no matter the coaxing. 'He always wanted to help others. He gave us everything when he was alive. Even in death, he has left us something in terms of compensation,' Mitul says.

KAWAN THAKUR

Loved cartoons and wanted to learn animation

For a mother who has lost her youngest son to a mindless act of terror, Salma Thakur is very brave. These days, two months after Kawan (19) died in the 7/11 train blasts, she is determined not to brood. 'I have enough beautiful memories of my son to see me through the rest of my life,' she says. That day, Kawan was coming home later than usual. After classes at the Hinduja College were over in the morning – (he was a second-year junior college student studying commerce) – he'd decided to spend some time with friends in town as he did not have his usual accountancy classes in the evening. Kawan was an avid lover of cartoon films. And even though he would fight like a baby, especially with his two older sisters Priya and Puja, for control over television time, he was, in fact, quite mature for his age. Brother Deepak can vouch for that. Having lost their father, Suhas Thakur, a photographer, five years back, the siblings are all quite mature and responsible for their age. 'Kawan was fully aware of the hardships the family faced,' says his mother. 'That's why he wasn't keen on completing his commerce degree. He wanted to take up a computer animation course. That way he could earn money for the family.' Kawan had another interest. He was keen to build his body. And even though his sisters teased him about it, he joined a gym. 'Kawan wanted to build his muscles. All of us laughed at him but he was determined to go ahead,' recalls Deepak fondly. 'Unlike his peers, he was pretty big for his age. All of us remember Kawan for his amiable nature and his sporting attitude.'

Omkarnath Mishra

Amway distributor, he was all set to travel to Europe

Anirudh's father Omkarnath Mishra (45), a distributor for Amway International, died on July 11 in the blast at Borivali railway station. Being a marketing man, Omkarnath was always on the move. Until 7.40 pm that day, his family had assumed that he was meeting a client, even though they had heard of the blasts. Then Omkarnath's younger brother Jayprakash got a call from his elder brother's cell phone. Omkarnath – wrongly listed as Omprakash – had sustained injuries to the back of his head, his left palm and ear. 'His face, shirt, trousers, socks, everything was intact. Except, he was dead,' says Jayprakash. 'At the morgue, blood was flowing as if it were a river.' Omkarnath's family remembers him as a man of few words. 'He would not mingle with people. He was focused on his work and home, that's all. We have been living here for four years, but hardly anyone knows him. He would always mind his own business,' says son Anirudh. Eldest of four children, Omkarnath came to Mumbai in 1983 after he cleared his Standard XII exams in Jaunpur, Uttar Pradesh. He did a few odd jobs initially while staying with his uncle at Khar, but soon made contacts and started a business of his own. A couple of years ago, he became an Amway distributor. 'Since then it had been a path of growth for him. He was very hard-working. Ask anyone at the Landmark building in Andheri, and they will tell you stories about my brother's work ethic,' says Jayprakash.

VITHAL CHOUDHARY

Was his young son's boxing partner

Young Praful's smile is what separates him from the rest of the neighbourhood children. Just nine, he smiles easily as he talks about his school grades and eagerly shares anecdotes and his hobbies. These days though, he uses that generous smile 'more as a shield', say family members. According to his mother Kavita, ever since he lost father Vithal Choudhary (46) to the July 11 blasts at Borivali station, Praful has 'suddenly become a man'. Choudhary, a senior section engineer at the Bombay Central office of Western Railway, was returning home to take the family shopping that evening. An affectionate man, he was little Praful's best friend too. On the night of July 11, when the family finally found Choudhary's blood-soaked body at Bhagwati hospital, it was Praful who consoled Choudhary's father-in-law, his grandfather Vinayak Vatkar. 'He insisted that he wanted to see his father, against our wishes. He finally peeped into the mortuary and looked at his father's face,' says the 66-year-old Vatkar. 'After that, there was a calm within him. It was I who could not rein in my emotions.' The child misses his boxing partner, something that's repeated several times during the conversation, alongside details such as the last best score his dad earned in Solitaire. Kavita fondly recalls her husband's favourite morning habit: reading four newspapers, then making a cup of tea for her. By 6 am, Praful would be wide awake too, launching boxing contests with his father and disturbing his reading. Little wonder, then, that Praful did not like newspapers – they ate into his fun-time with his father.

Harshal Bhalerao

Cricket enthusiast, it was his first day at work

'Every day, when I cross Borivali station, I silently weep,' says Yashwant Bhalerao, who works at the Mantralaya. Harshal (23) was his only child. Bhalerao himself was on another train bombed that day – at Mira-Bhayander station. Fortunately, he wasn't in the coach in which the bomb went off. Harshal was returning from the software firm in Andheri he had joined. He had told his mother he would be late, but work ended early that day. On the way he had planned to pick up his certificates from college, but changed his mind and headed home instead. 'He must have been bursting to tell us about his first day at work,' says Bhalerao. 'But our dreams crashed like a house of cards. Now we have nothing to plan for, nothing to look forward to. We are surviving on a day-to-day basis with his memories.' 'Dynamic and popular, with a creative mind and a positive attitude' – that's how Harshal's cousins Swapnil and Vishal, who live in the Bhalerao home at Vasai, remember him. Harshal had just completed his computer management diploma at K.C. College after a degree in commerce. He had bagged a job at a software firm only a month ago. 'When he got the job, he was very happy. He kept telling us he wanted to build his own identity and then help us do the same. We relied on his vision, but now we feel helpless,' says Swapnil. 'His knowledge of cricket was amazing,' adds Vishal. 'You had to just show him a clip, he could exactly tell you which match was being played, where it was being played, and who had scored how much. He himself was a fantastic player and played at the local club level.'

Kamlesh Ashar

A keen badminton player, he was saving to buy a car

Kamlesh Ashar (34) had big plans for Ravison, his brand of snacks and namkeen. And since he supplied to call centres and the new commercial centres in Malad and Goregaon, Mumbai's local trains played a significant role in his business. A commerce graduate from Somaiya College in Ghatkopar, Kamlesh, along with his mother Rajani and sister Dharini, had moved out of his small home in Ghatkopar to a relatively spacious one-bedroom flat in Vasai, a decade ago. Having lost his father Ravidas when he was just four and Dharini just a baby, Kamlesh had braved some tough times. Rajani, who has a teaching degree, ran the household on her earnings as a tutor. Now, sitting alone in their quiet home, Rajani remembers her fun-loving son's enthusiasm and dreams of the good life. 'He wanted to buy a car this Diwali,' says the forlorn mother. 'He'd started taking driving lessons just a week before the blasts.' Kamlesh, who separated from wife Dhrupali four years ago, was a careful spender, however. He didn't even travel first class until he gave in to his mother's insistence two months before the blasts. The Navratri festivities bring back special memories, for Kamlesh was popular in the neighbourhood for his jocular nature and his love for the dandiya nights. A keen badminton player, the other big unwinding ritual for Kamlesh was to spend time with his family. After work every day, he'd discuss the day's events with Rajani. 'On Sundays, he would help me cook,' his mother recalls fondly.

Babulal Waghani

Diamond trader, he moved to Mumbai for his children's sake

That day, for some reason, Babulal Waghani (36) left home later than usual. Nearly three months on, his wife Ranjan doesn't want to let go of those last 30 minutes they spent together. She doesn't want to believe he's gone. *'Kya milta hai unko bekasur logon ko mar kar ke? Hum to apni mehnat ki kamayi karke apni zindagi jee rahe the,'* she says, sitting listlessly on a sofa at her Borivali residence. Babulal grew up in a village near Vapi in Gujarat. After finishing primary school, he shifted to Surat to help his uncle in his business. Eldest among four siblings, he did odd jobs initially, then entered the diamond business in Surat and soon found his feet. Marriage happened, weekly trips to Mumbai in search of better business followed. Then, five years ago, he shifted to Mumbai. He had studied only till class X, but had big plans for his two sons, Kamal and Piyush. 'He wanted them to go to English-medium schools, speak in English, and get a good education,' says Ranjan. On July 10, Kamal got a seat in Mithibai College for a commerce degree. The next day, hours before the blasts, he had his last conversation with his father. 'He had called me to tell me that I had been listed for the science stream at Jai Hind College. He left the choice to me, but before we could take any decision, this happened. Now even if I want to do science, I will lose a year. I may as well do commerce,' says Kamal. The Waghanis cheer up a little when they recall the good times – how Babulal would cook them Sunday lunches or take them to the movies – the last movie they watched together was *36 China Town*.

Rajesh Damodar Pandrekar

Young software specialist, took on the family's duties

Thirteen years ago, when Damodar Pandrekar underwent heart surgery, his eldest son Rajesh, then 20, told him: 'Bhau, you need to rest now, you need to retire. This home is now my responsibility.' A police constable, Pandrekar quit his job and Rajesh quit his studies. Since then, he had been the family's breadwinner, working for a marine engineering firm. 'He was so young, but he understood so much. And he was a fighter till the end,' says his bereaved father. 'Our pillar has suddenly disappeared. He worked for us, lived for us. He was the ideal big brother,' says Naresh, youngest of the three brothers, recalling how Rajesh (33) – who had worked up to a software specialist's position at his firm – always told his siblings to focus on their studies and leave earning money to him. 'He was unlike us. After work, he would head straight for home. But if we wanted to eat out he would quickly agree and take us there. He never said no,' adds Dinesh. If his family relied on him for everything, so did several relatives whenever they needed help, especially on occasions like weddings. Then too, Rajesh never refused any of them. His mother Surekha was looking forward to getting him married. But Rajesh insisted that marriage could wait. 'He was too busy working. Often, to earn overtime, he would wake up at 3.30 am and leave for office by 5 am. I would always tell him not to overwork, but he would reply, "I am doing this for all of you,"' says Surekha, sobbing as she stares at her son's photograph.

187 MUMBAI LIFE STORIES

AMITABH LAXMINARAYAN PAI

A bank executive who loved animals

Once, as a schoolboy, he pestered his mother to buy a pair of parakeets, only to set them free. On another occasion, he spent weeks nursing an injured squirrel. And till the day before he died, he fed a bowl of rice and milk to the stray dog that had made the staircase to the family's apartment its home. Amitabh Laxminarayan Pai loved animals. 'He was so kind that given a chance, he would not have borne a grudge even against the people who bombed his train at Jogeshwari station on July 11,' says his elder sister Nilima, tears welling up in her eyes. 'Chintu had set his sights on a bigger flat so he could keep an Alsatian,' says Amitabh's mother Maya. 'He wanted to buy all the comforts for me and his father,' she adds, pointing to the 29-inch TV and air conditioner that Amitabh had bought on instalments when he started working. Only 27, Amitabh was the youngest of three siblings and was doing well after earning a commerce degree. With two promotions in a year, he had reached the managerial level in the customer support department of the ICICI's Webtrade office at Prabhadevi. He had been on that job for nearly three years. But he wanted to achieve more and had enrolled for evening MBA classes at the Mumbai Educational Trust in Bandra where he had done well in the first two years of the three-year programme. Amitabh also wanted to live a good life. 'He was crazy about watches and branded clothes,' says Nilima, pulling out a beige case containing more than a dozen watches from under Amitabh's bed. Often, on Sundays, he would rustle up Hakka noodles and fried rice for the entire family.

DINESH SOLANKI

He put off marriage to look after his family

On July 11, Dinesh (30) was in a hurry to get home to distant Nallasopara. He had worked hard all day and was hungry. Before leaving office, he called his mother telling her to make a snack for him. 'If only he had waited for his colleagues another five minutes, he might have been alive today,' says Dinesh's mother Jamuna Solanki. He worked as an office boy at Job Track, a placement agency at Mahim, a job he'd had for three years. Younger brother Hemant had quit his job only four months before the blasts, which meant Dinesh and Jamuna, a midwife, were the only earning members of a family of six. Hemant describes his brother as a very meticulous person, careful about his appearance and clothing despite his modest job. 'He was also fond of perfumes,' says Hemant. 'He was supposed to go for a haircut that evening.' He may have had a weakness for trendy haircuts but Dinesh knew what he could afford. The first class pass was a recent acquisition, which his employers had sponsored. 'We couldn't afford a first class season ticket, but Dinesh's boss suggested that he should travel by first class,' says Jamuna. At 30, Dinesh was still single, something family members point to as proof of his commitment to them. Apparently, despite years of cajoling by relatives, he had resolutely refused to get married because the family's financial position was far from secure. But Dinesh had finally agreed – his job was satisfying and future prospects bright. The family had been looking around for a suitable bride and the wedding would have been slated for the end of the year.

DILIP KEWAT

Coordinator at Asian Institute of Management, he was content

Sunita has told her sons that their father is in Manila. Dilip Kewat (33) travelled often and the five-year-old twins are used to his long absences. But this time they sense something's wrong. 'They play hide-and-seek around me when they see me crying or talking about my husband to someone, just to eavesdrop on what I reveal,' says Sunita, before younger twin Omkaar enters the room. Omkaar's headmistress had met Sunita just a week ago to say how the 'naughty boy' nowadays slumps on the bench with moist eyes, and does not even open his tiffin box. The other twin, Pratamesh, wants to know why, these days, so many strangers visit their seventh-floor apartment on Mira Road and enquire about their father. Dilip worked as a co-ordinator for the Asian Institute of Management, which is headquartered in Manila. On July 11, he was returning home in the first class coach of the train that was bombed at Borivali station. Sunita, a science graduate, and Dilip fell in love when they were in college. He was a year senior. She remembers how Dilip, 'a very shy person', proposed to her: 'It just happened. There was never any formal exchange of words, we just knew that we were meant for each other.' As a co-ordinator for AMI, Dilip was always on the cell phone, sometimes even late in the night. Sunita smiles as she recalls how Dilip had reacted after the doctor told him that he had become a father of twins. '"My God, how will I manage two?" he had asked,' she says. But he did and the twins adored him. 'Papa was everything for them,' says Sunita.

Pravinkumar Upadhyay

Accountant, taught his family to be self-reliant

July 11 began on a happy note for the Upadhyays. Pravinkumar (55) had returned from Baroda early in the morning, a day earlier than planned. Together they had watched a video of his younger son Mehul's wedding, that had been held recently. The CDs had been delivered only the day before, and the family was waiting for Pravinkumar to be back. 'We were so happy. We had no idea what the day had in store for us,' recalls son Tejas, the eldest of three siblings. The youngest is his sister Preeti. An accountant, Pravinkumar managed the book-keeping for all the group companies of Central Automobiles on Charni Road. He had been with the firm for 29 years. At 8.30 am on July 11, Pravinkumar left for office. Eleven hours later, his family heard of the blasts. Nearly three months on, Tejas regrets two things his father missed out on: the first long vacation he had planned with his family, later that month, and his promotion as the company's chief accountant, due later that year. A 'strict disciplinarian' Pravinkumar trained the Upadhyays 'to be self-reliant'. He even taught his children how to maintain account books at an early age. Born in a village in Gujarat, Pravinkumar had dreams of a decent life and it was in Mumbai that he decided to pursue them. Decades of hard work had taken a toll on Pravinkumar's health and, in May last year, he had to undergo an angioplasty. 'We told him to take voluntary retirement. But my father was a restless person and work was an integral part of his life,' says Tejas.

187 MUMBAI LIFE STORIES

Prabhakar Ghume

Insurance agent; his wife now struggles to cope

'Daddy will come home for Diwali' – that's eight-year-old Sayli's simple explanation for her father's absence from the Ghume family's quiet household in Virar. Prabhakar Ghume (37) died on July 11 in the blast in a packed local train at Matunga station. And little Sayli has been her mother Aparna's biggest support since. 'She sometimes wipes my tears and says he will come back and play with her in the garden,' says Aparna. An insurance agent with the Life Insurance Corporation for 13 years, Prabhakar commuted every day between Churchgate and Virar, an hour-and-a-half ride. That fatal Tuesday, he'd decided against attending an evening meeting at his office and chosen to return home early. Prabhakar was the oldest of five siblings. Three brothers and a sister are now constantly by Aparna's side but finances are a problem. That's an irony, say family members, as Prabhakar would often help clients who couldn't pay up insurance premiums on time, while his own last premium was overdue. 'I still haven't received the insurance money,' Aparna says. 'There are certain formalities to be completed. I have written a letter to LIC.' Prabhakar and Aparna, both from Mumbai, were married nine years ago. For seven years, they lived in a rented home at Nallasopara. Two years ago, the Ghumes had moved to their new flat in Virar, a humble affair, but one his wife is immensely proud of. 'The day we moved to this house was the happiest in our lives. We felt very secure here, Prabhakar was so happy,' Aparna recalls.

Rohit Kumar Jain

Gemology student and incorrigible TV gameshow hopeful

Any contest on the TV, Internet or mobile phone, and Rohit (21) would SMS away. He often won something, but his last success was big: Rs 1 lakh for questions on the movie *Kabhi Alvida Na Kehna*. 'His friends used to tease him, saying at this rate he wouldn't need a job,' says Rohit's mother Anita Jain. But on July 11, fate had other plans. Rohit was returning home from the International Gemological Institute on Charni Road, where he was studying 'everything about diamonds'. When the train reached Borivali station, a bomb went off in his coach. He was seriously injured and died in hospital. About 45 minutes before the explosion, when the train was crossing Charni Road station, he had called his mother to say he was on his way. 'I had cooked his favourite arbi, raita and paneer,' says Anita, as she breaks down clutching his photograph. An only child, Rohit was the centre of his parents' world. So when they bought a new two-bedroom apartment in Bhayander in February, they 'kept his tastes and future in mind'. Says his father Surendra Jain: 'Soon, he would have started working and would have needed more space. And one day, he would have got married. Our old one-bedroom flat was too small.' Rohit's institute was planning to send him to Belgium next year for a special course in diamonds. His big dream was to design diamond jewellery and one day run his own boutique. 'He loved the good life. He bought his clothes from malls, always wore branded stuff, and enjoyed Italian and Chinese food,' says his father. 'I had not done any of that, but I wanted him to.'

Tushit Shah

A positive attitude saw him through hardship

Two years before the blast at Jogeshwari station snatched Tushit Shah (44) away from his family, he had asked them: 'What would you do if I died or went away somewhere?' His wife Meeta had replied with words of admonition. It was only when Tushit broke into '*Tera peechha na main chhodoonga soniye*' – one of his favourite Kishore Kumar numbers – that she had relented and smiled. 'He said if he was reborn, he would want to marry me again but this time, it would be after a long courtship, not in the placid, arranged manner we had wed 19 years ago,' says Meeta of her doting husband. 'He was always so positive about everything,' she says, recalling how he had pulled through many years of hardship to reach a satisfying point in his career. His optimistic outlook has also inspired her with the strength to go on and take care of their teenaged daughter Esha. After studying science at Don Bosco school, Borivali, and textile engineering at St Xavier's College, Tushit faced many setbacks while trying to establish a textile business. It was after many long years of struggle that he found his calling, dabbling in shares trading. He worked as an institutional sales trader at TAIB securities, a subsidiary of Dubai-based TAIB Bank, before he shifted to BRICS securities, Worli, as an institutional equity dealer this May. Even in the short time he worked there, he became popular. And he leaves a lot of goodwill behind. Now wife Meeta, a psychologist, has organized a '7/11 group'. She meets often with the other widows of the blasts, and together they give each other counsel, comfort and courage.

Pramod Vispute

Mechanical engineer and a stickler for punctuality

Pramod Vispute(42) was a stickler for efficiency and punctuality. So, on July 11, when he didn't come home and his family couldn't get through to his cell phone all evening, they feared the worst. A mechanical engineer, Pramod worked as a marketing manager for a private firm in Andheri. Some of his colleagues had waited for peak hour to pass, to get a less crowded train, but he boarded the train because he wanted to reach home on time, as always. When his body was brought home, his two-year-old son Aditya was told that 'Daddy is asleep'. 'Aditya is now like my own son,' says brother Umesh, who has two sons. Pramod's wife Priya is away, at her maternal home, where she went soon after the tragedy. 'I sent her there for 15-20 days, hoping it would help her overcome the grief,' says Umesh. Aditya was with her too, but the extended family had decided that the Vasai home was too dull without his bubbly presence and brought him back. 'Now, suddenly, the house is cheerful once again,' says Umesh. Pramod and Umesh were close, having lived in the Vasai home together for 23 years, even after both got married and the family grew. Umesh vows he will look after his brother's family now. 'Priya is like my little sister,' he says. Both brothers were self-made men, having achieved positions of respect after years of struggle. Pramod even worked part-time while studying for his engineering degree, says Umesh. 'He did everything with great efficiency.' Other relatives agree: Pramod was 'immensely well-organized'.

Hriday Naikwade

Electronics postgraduate, playwright, journalist

His passion for theatre brought him to Mumbai ten years ago. He was sure his two Masters degrees in electronics and physics would get him a job anywhere. And the stage in Akola, where Hriday Naikwade (38) grew up and studied, was too small to chase his passion. In Mumbai, as he wrote plays and watched performances, he pursued something new: a diploma in mass communications and journalism. Hours before the blasts on July 11, he called his wife Katha at their Virar home to tell her the results had just been announced and he had scored 70 per cent. Katha knew Hriday was in south Mumbai for some work, but didn't know when he'd be returning home. She didn't hear from him again. 'Even after a long day at work, he would pitch in any way,' says Katha, a name given to her by Hriday. 'In fact, I had to insist that he should go and rest or watch TV, but he wouldn't.' Married soon after her post-graduation – she is an MSc (Maths) and gives tuitions to schoolchildren – Katha was uncertain about matrimony at the age of 22. But looking back, she has 'no regrets', she says. 'Hriday made the transition so easy, it was so comfortable. He was more like a friend than a husband.' After daughter Nimritee's birth, Hriday took it upon himself to help out in every possible way. Katha says creative writing was in the family, and Hriday's poetry was as good as his drama. His themes centred around the 'one moment that completely changes one's life', she says, now thinking of the irony of it.

GERALD FERNANDES

Real estate consultant, who recently had the house renovated

Years ago, when their families lived in Kalina, Gerald and Ignacinha used to take bus No. 315 to Mahim church every Sunday. Though there was a stop near his house, Gerald would walk down to the one where Ignacinha would be waiting with her parents. 'One day I asked him why he did that,' says Ignacinha. 'He replied: "This is a free country, I can choose whichever bus stop I want to."' Soon, love blossomed. Then, one day, Gerald left for Dubai. 'Everyone told me to get married. But I waited for him. I knew he would come back to marry me,' says Ignacinha, 39. One thing that still baffles her three months after 7/11 is why Gerald (45), who never returned home before 10 pm, chose to leave early that day. And why he boarded the first first class coach when he always took the one at the end of the train. Ignacinha vividly remembers their last few moments together on the morning of July 11. A supervisor for the real estate company Integrated Property Management and Services at Worli, Gerald was getting ready to leave for work. 'I noticed three strands of hair on his shirt and told him he was losing hair,' says Ignacinha. 'He laughed and told me to get some oil which would stop it. I said I would get Kerala ayurvedic oil.' She says she finds it difficult to accept that he's no more: 'I still clean up the hall in the evening, as he used to get annoyed if it looked messy. I often feel he'll come home.' Only recently, Gerald had had got their modest house renovated 'for no apparent reason'. 'He simply said that it's been 14 years since we bought it and it looked old,' says Ignacinha.

Abhinav Srivastava

Tailor, came to work in Mumbai two weeks ago

When Abhinav Srivastava (25) left his house at Nallasopara on July 11, he was heading for the post-funeral rites of his uncle in a village near hometown Varanasi. But fate had a devious plan. On his way to board the outbound train from Dadar Terminus, he alighted at Santa Cruz on an afterthought to call up his father Harischandra, who lives in Varanasi. His father told him he wanted Abhinav to visit relatives in Virar and personally inform them about the function on the 13th day after the death of his uncle Rajaram. After talking to his father, Abhinav turned back towards Virar in a local train. His wife Anita, who was at home in Nallasopara had assumed that he was on his way to Varanasi. Abhinav was a tailor, who had come to Mumbai only in the last week of June. He had found a job at a garment factory in Lower Parel, and lived with Anita and their three-year-old daughter Tanya in a simple flat in Nallasopara, owned by his parents-in-law. 'Though he'd worked here for just a fortnight, he already had plans to buy his own house and settle down in Mumbai; he had come with a dream,' says his wife. Kailash Srivastava, principal of a primary school in Nallasopara who is married to Anita's sister, says: 'He was always well-mannered and courteous. He always longed only to be with his wife and daughter.' Much of what Anita remembers of her five-year arranged marriage to Abhinav are her troubles with her in-laws and long periods spent at her parents' home. Still, despite their problems, Abhinav was always soft-spoken, never one to be caught in an argument.

Ramdas Shirodkar

Graphic designer who was both boss and friend to his son

On July 26, 2005, when Mumbai's railway tracks went under several inches of water, Ramdas Shirodkar (52) walked 40 kilometres from Churchgate to Bhayander before taking a rickshaw to his home in Vasai. So on July 11, his wife Archana thought he was caught up in something similar. But the next day, Archana's sister Nilima Wagle found his body at Tunga hospital on Mira Road. Ramdas was listed as unidentified because all his belongings had been stolen. When Nilima reached the hospital, the staff were about to move his body to Thane. Ramdas last spoke to Archana at 1.30 pm that Tuesday. 'Every day, he would call me after lunch and tell me to have mine. I would never eat before his call,' she says. 'As soon as we heard of the blasts, we started calling his cell phone, but he was unreachable. I then tried calling our son Yuvraj and got through to him. He informed me that he was safe.' Ramdas worked for a private firm, Anchor Electric Beauty Care, in Lower Parel as its creative head. His son Yuvraj, 23, works as a graphic designer in the same company. 'He was my boss, friend and father,' he says. On July 11, after work, Yuvraj had travelled separately to reach Sion for his 3D graphics classes. Four days after Ramdas died the Shirodkars realized that someone had stolen Rs 32,000 from his bank account. 'Papa had written the password of his ATM account on a paper in his wallet,' says daughter Deepti. Besides the Shirodkar family, his dog Oscar and cats Montu and Chingi are lost without him; they didn't eat any food for a week after he died.

From Tuesday 4 July. 10pm
AKELA

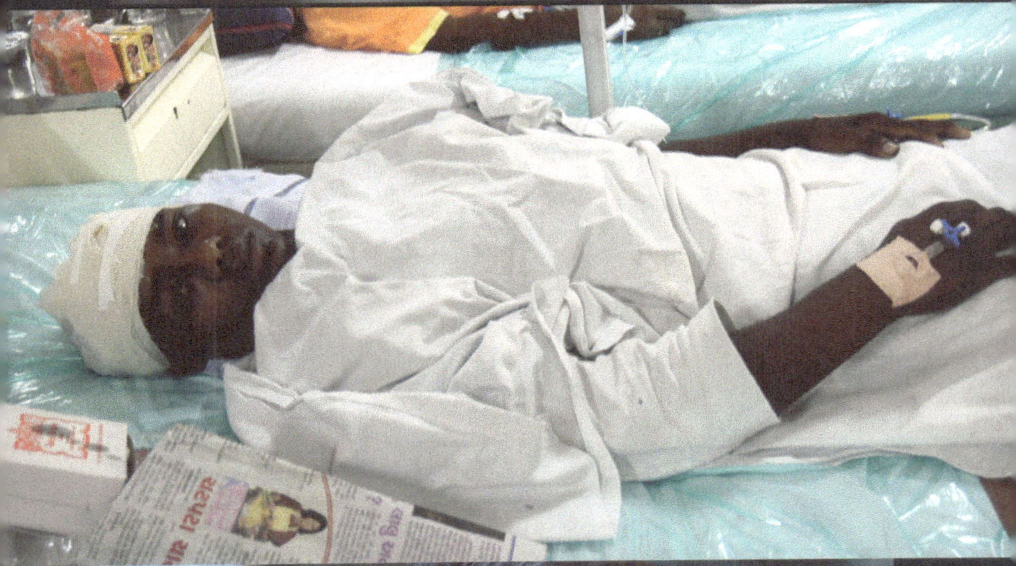

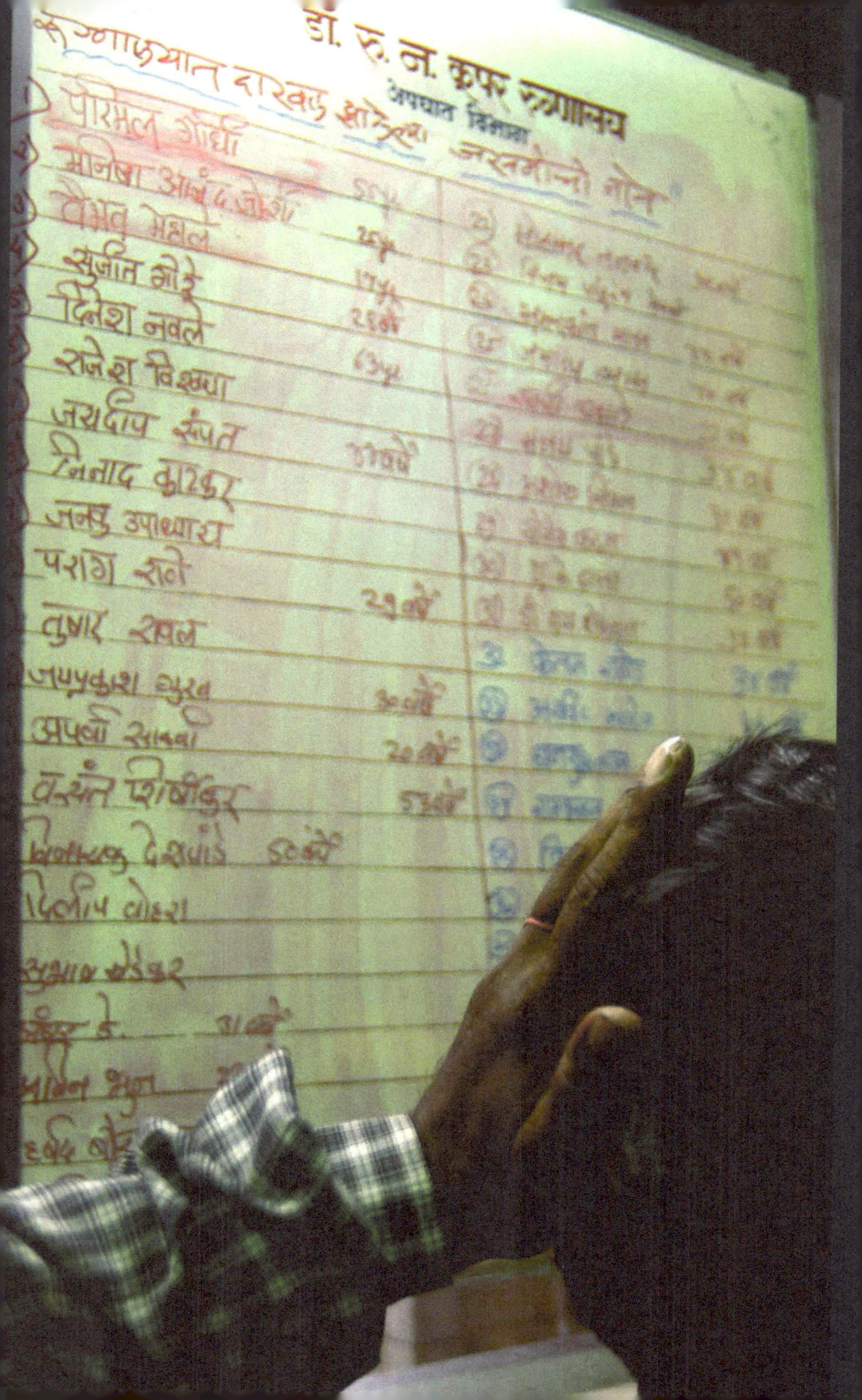
डा. रु. न. कूपर रुग्णालय
अपघात विभाग
रुग्णालयात दाखल झालेल्या जखमींची नावे

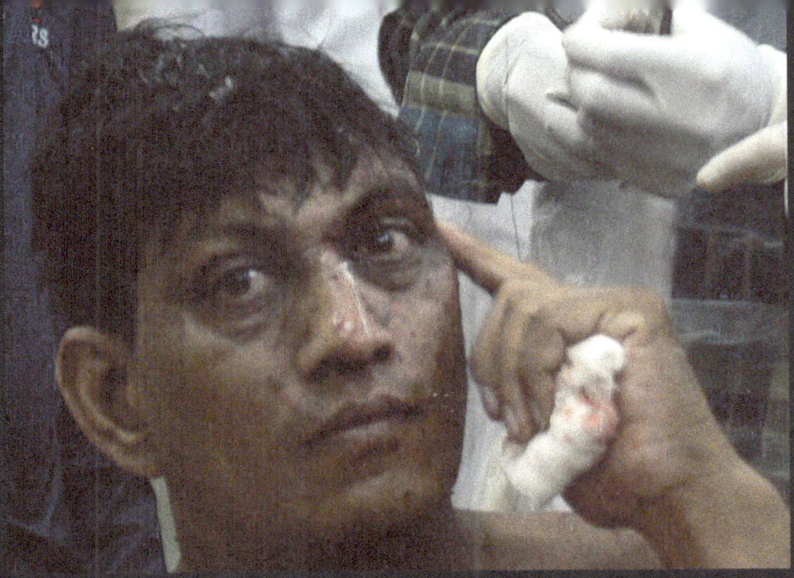

0547

843

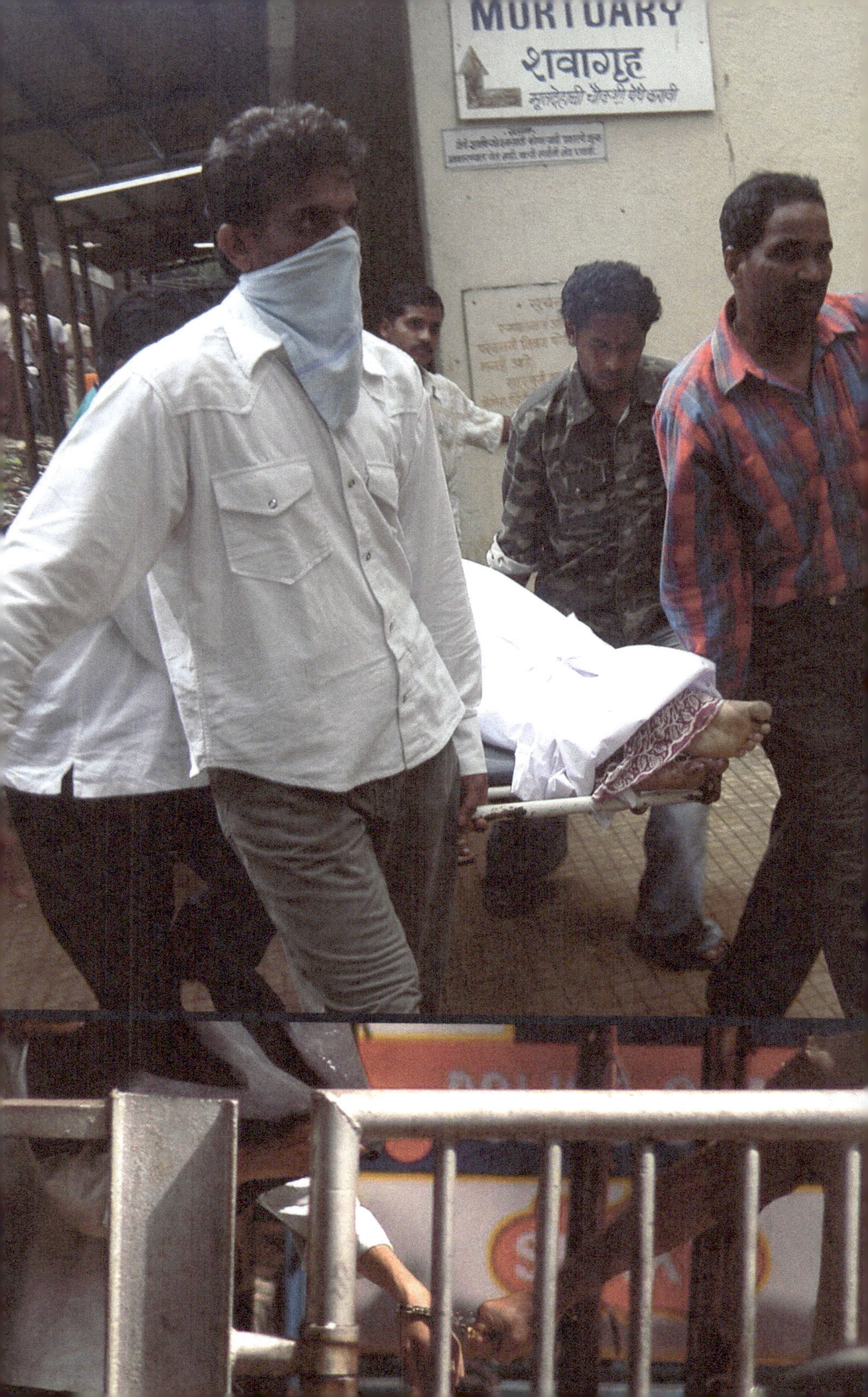
MORTUARY
शवागृह

WESTERN

FIRST CLASS

187 MUMBAI LIFE STORIES

Nitin Patil

Bank clerk from Jalgaon; was at home in the city

'He wanted me to wear jeans, but I never did. That wish remains to be fulfilled.' Three months after 7/11 left her widowed, Prawara finds solace in talking about how her husband Nitin (37) was the one who groomed her for Mumbai. She cut her waist-long tresses to a boyish bob soon after marriage, started using lipstick and got her eyebrows done regularly. These days Prawara finds comfort in attributing this introduction to 'posh living' to Nitin's broad-mindedness. But it didn't start off easily. Brought up in a conservative Maharashtrian family, Prawara remembers her shock when, days after their wedding, Nitin asked her to say hello to his friends. 'Growing up in Jalgaon, I remember how my father said that a girl should always keep a distance from men,' she explains. 'First, I thought it was Bombay,' she says. But she soon realized just how liberal her husband was, considering his humble roots. These fond memories have been cruelly disturbed by the traumatic experience of that Tuesday. Nitin had dreams of his own and was working hard to realize them as a clerk at the Maharashtra State Cooperative Bank. Having dropped out of college a year after taking up post-graduation in commerce, he left his hometown Jalgaon to come to Mumbai in search of work. In the early days, he would juggle work at the bank to be personal assistant to his MLA uncle, Vijay Naval Patil. This went on for about three years but marriage meant he had to quit working for his uncle to focus on his job and family. Says Prawara, 'He was employed as a clerk, but did the work of a junior officer.'

AJAY SEVADA

The household whizkid whom every one turned to for advice

Ajay (19) was the youngest in the family. Yet, when it came to seeking advice for all things big and small, even his 48-year-old father Daulatram would consult him.'We could never have imagined a life without Ajju, as he was fondly called,' says elder brother Vimal. 'He was the blue-eyed boy of the family.' Three months after the 7/11 train blasts, the six-member Sevada family in Borivali is still trying its best to deal with that unimaginable reality. They remember him every day, talk about him, share anecdotes and finally, find solace in the thought that if Ajay had lived he would have realized his dreams. 'He was precise and articulate. He never spoke for the sake of speaking. Whatever he said made sense and that's why we all sought advice from him,' says Vimal. Ajay was serious, responsible and methodical in his studies. Vimal doesn't recall a single occasion when his younger brother had to be told to study. 'During his higher secondary, he made his own study time-table beginning at 4 am and winding up for the day around midnight,' he says. 'He was the brightest of us all. Anybody who got admission to the University Institute of Chemical Technology (UICT) has to be.' Living in a small Maharashtra Housing Board apartment on Gorai Road, Ajay had big dreams. He wanted to pursue his post-graduation on scholarship in London. And he was confident he would make the grade. 'He never said he hoped to get the scholarship. He was sure he would get it,' adds Vimal, who believes that if fate had allowed his brother another ten years 'he would have definitely become a role model like, say, Kalpana Chawla.'

Mukundrai Amidas Modi

Businessman, was planning a holiday in Europe during Diwali

Mukundrai Amidas Modi's family wants the government to ensure that the 7/11 case does not drag on for 13 years like the 1993 serial blasts trial. 'All we want is a quick judgment because justice delayed is justice denied,' says his son Mukesh. 'The blast has taken my father away 15 years early. It's an irreparable loss,' he adds, stressing that at 71, Mukundrai was a very fit person and rarely fell ill. Mukundrai was born in a village in Saurashtra and shifted to Mumbai when he was 15. Years of hard work bore fruit when he started the now well-established Praful Stationeries at Churchgate, presently managed by his sons. 'My father was very attached to the family business. Despite his retirement, he made it a point to attend office every day to supervise and help us,' says Mukesh, second of Mukundrai's three sons. He was equally fond of eating out and travelling. In fact, he was planning to tour Europe this Diwali and 'was very excited about it'. On July 11, Mukundrai, 'an extremely disciplined man', followed his daily routine: taking an hour-long morning walk before setting off to work. Only, that day, he left late because he had to attend the housing society's meeting. Family and neighbours remember having requested him to stay at home and rest for the day since he was feeling unwell. '*Janey do, nahin to mere betey akele pad jayenge,*' he had told his grand-daughter Shruti. He left office around 5.30 pm as usual. When the train reached Jogeshwari station, the bomb went off. His family heard about the blasts, but assumed he was safe as he normally stopped at the local temple on his way home.

Krishnakumar Dubey

Scientist, was using his first class pass for the first time

If you said you liked something of his, he would immediately gift it to you. That, says Krishnakumar Dubey's wife, Anita, is what gave him the most pleasure. He also loved his job as a scientist and enjoyed taking pictures of his family. But these days, when his three-year-old son Utkarsh sees his father in the video clip of his last birthday, he asks for him and Anita doesn't know what to say. 'I was really excited about last Diwali's gift,' says Anita. 'He bought the latest Handycam and camera phone to click our pictures and shoot family videos on special occasions.' If Krishnakumar (36) loved giving gifts, the railway pass was his gift to himself. Even Anita didn't know he had got himself one and that he would be using it that day. He died while returning home from work. Working as a scientist handling intellectual property rights at Wockhardt in Bandra, Krishnakumar had been recently promoted to senior scientist. Personally, too, he was a contented man, reveals Anita. The Dubeys had bought themselves a new apartment a few months before and were to move out of their rented Kandivali house soon. Now, Anita doesn't want to live in Mumbai anymore. Uppermost on her mind is Utkarsh's future. 'I am leaving this city for Delhi by next month. We cannot afford to pay such high rent for this flat,' says Anita. She remembers seeing him off that day. 'Like always, I was standing in the balcony to wave him goodbye. He would continue to wave till he disappeared into the distance. That was his habit. How was I to know that would be his last goodbye to me?' says Anita, for the first time unable to hold back her tears.

Ajit Pangle

Peon with MTNL, had a son two months ago

Apart from the happiness that comes with the birth of a son in a middle-class household, Ajit Pangle (30) was also relieved: at last he had someone who would fulfil his own unfulfilled ambitions. And so, even when Soham was only two months old, Ajit's worry was how to get him admitted to a good school, get him through high school and then put him in college. 'He was determined to give him the right kind of education,' says his wife Jhanvi. 'He had plans to make him an engineer, a reputed person in society.' Being a peon with MTNL weighed heavily on Ajit. And he always tried to prove himself by doing more than what he was expected to. So he took the trouble of learning computers and became well-versed in the basics of Microsoft Office applications. 'He may have been a peon, but he was good enough in computers to handle his boss's work,' says mother Urmila. 'His boss told us he was a bright boy.' Maybe that's why MTNL has now decided to take care of one year's instalments of Ajit's home loan of Rs 4 lakh. But ever since Ajit died in the 6.29 pm Virar blast while returning home to Bhayander, the family worries about this debt constantly. Still, they try not to talk about the things that worry them. Instead, they talk about the good times. 'We were very close. All four of us played a lot of hide-and-seek and everyone knew where he would hide,' recalls Swati fondly about the time when the four siblings were together. 'Ajit was unlucky as he didn't have much of a childhood after his father died. He had to give up studies midway so that his brother and two sisters could continue to study,' says his mother.

187 MUMBAI LIFE STORIES

Naishat Ramniklal Tejani

Had bought a new car but took the train

About a month before 7/11, Naishat (44) had bought a Santro car and was using it to go to work. That day, he decided enough was enough. Mumbai's potholed roads were not worth it. So he took the train. Today, many months after the Mahim train blast killed him, the family is yet to pick up the pieces. Wife Jayshree is angry at the state's indifference, but her larger worry is the future of the children, daughter Kinjal and son Apurva. 'I am an MA in sociology but have never had to work. After my marriage, my husband told me that the children would need someone at home.' Young Apurva disapproves of any talk of his mother going out to work. 'He is not allowing me to work,' she says applying balm on his forehead to ease his headache. 'He says, "If a bomb kills you, we will have no one to take care of us."' Naishat was particular about his health and fitness. He practised yoga every day. 'He had also made sure that we also practised it. He would call me and say, "If Kinjal doesn't perform yoga today, don't give her lunch,"' recalls Jayshree. His colleagues at Bluestar, where he used to work, vouch for his health obsession. 'I spent a lot of time with him when we were in New Delhi for about six months last year. He would tell us about the virtues of yogasana and a vegetarian diet,' says Pramod Patil, who has since changed his own lifestyle due to Naishat's influence and is now pushing his family to follow suit. Naishat was a straightforward person, who didn't mince his words. And that's what endeared him to his friends and colleagues.

Himanshu Buddhadev

A responsible man and Bachchan fan

Memories are all Dhwani has. After all, they were to celebrate their first wedding anniversary in Goa on July 15. And since that wasn't to be, these days she finds comfort in sharing some happy stories about her husband, Himanshu (25). Like the time he pushed through a crowd to meet his idol Amitabh Bachchan, his fondness for sweets, and his unfulfilled dream of buying a new car. 'I would always tease him that he was incapable of pulling off a surprise. That day, he gave me the biggest surprise of my life,' says Dhwani. On July 11 Himanshu left his office at Mangal Das Market in the Marine Lines area earlier than usual. 'He called up his father, Prakashbhai, to tell him he was going to buy a surprise gift for me. He usually left office at 7:30 pm, but that day he left around 5:30 pm.' Dhwani believes Himanshu was fated to go. 'He would have left two hours earlier, had it not been for a visitor who showed up for some work unexpectedly,' she points out. Born and brought up in Mumbai, Himanshu studied in St. Xavier's School. 'As a child he was quite naughty,' says his mother Rashmiben. 'He would never enter the house unless I bought something for him after school. If I was away, he would refuse to enter the house and sat on the stairs for hours, waiting for me to return.' He was known for being a responsible boy too. Before he joined the family's cloth business, he got himself a diploma in import and export management from the Narsi Monjee Institute of Management Sciences. The elder of two brothers, Himanshu doted on his younger brother, Ankit.

Subhash Chotulal Shah

Thrilled with his daughter's success

Ever since the arrival of their only daughter, Alpa, in 1979, Subhash (54) had been nurturing one dream. Twenty-seven years old now, Alpa fulfilled that dream when she became a chartered accountant last year. And then, once her career was sorted out, all he and his wife Dharmishta would talk about was their daughter's marriage. 'We were a happy family, with Subhash and Alpa living like close buddies,' says Dharmishta. 'And when he would talk of Alpa's achievement it would be followed, almost invariably, by talk of her marriage. Then, there would be tears of joy in his eyes.' Both Alpa, who works in an accounting firm at Churchgate, and her mother have decided to remember Subhash for what he was and not for what happened to him. 'We have put away each and every picture of Subhash in the closet as that reminds us of 7/11 which we are trying hard to forget. We want to live with the fond memories and not the gory nightmares,' she says. Subhash worked from 9 am to 5 pm as a manager with a private firm in Ghatkopar, and spent all his spare time having a good time with his colleagues. So happy was he with his daughter's success that he would talk about it at every occasion. Those who knew him, swear by Subhash's love for life. More than anything else, he loved to share a great meal with his friends and family. Everyone in the locality knew him as one who took care to smile even at strangers. He was a contented man. Life was about equilibrium, Subhash would tell his wife, and he was balancing things just fine.

Ashok K. Ail

A cool, likeable young man

Five-year-old Shashank is now so frightened of trains that for the past three months he has been insisting on taking a bus or an autorickshaw every time he accompanies his mother Hema to some place. 'God is mad,' says Shashank. 'Didn't he know how much we need my papa? Please get him back from the sky.' His father, Ashok K. Ail (38) died in the bomb blast in a train between Mira Road and Bhayander stations on July 11. Ashok would have turned 39 on October 22. He was from a family of six brothers and sisters, and had struck out early on his own. As production manager, he oversaw the working of Roshan Tin Printers in Worli. Friends considered him 'cool' and colleagues liked him. 'He was a very helpful person. People who do not know about this incident still ask about him,' says wife Hema. Ashok loved watching movies and travelling. Only a fortnight before tragedy struck, the family had watched the Hrithik Roshan-starrer *Krrish*. In June, they had made a trip to Matheran, Nashik and Shirdi. 'He lived like a king,' remembers Hema. 'And he always wanted to live in the present, wanted to enjoy every moment of his life. "Who has seen tomorrow?" he would always say.' Hema's only subsistence for now is the cheque of six lakh rupees she has got as compensation from the railways. She has also applied for the job Western Railway has offered but since it is a Group D job – covering peons, helpers, cleaners, etc., – she is not too happy.

Rammilan Prajapati

A generous, helpful and neighbourly person

Friends and relatives will always remember Rammilan Prajapati (38) as a generous man. He was always there for them in times of need, helping out either with cash or in kind. So when they heard about his death on 7/11, many came to the funeral to bid him a last goodbye and used the opportunity to return to the family the money he had loaned them. 'Since he was so helpful, anyone who knew him would never think of cheating him,' says nephew Santosh K. Prajapati. 'That is why we were not surprised when people to whom he had given money voluntarily returned it.' For Santosh, Rammilan was more a brother than an uncle as the age difference between the two was only of a few years. Maybe that's why he is finding it so difficult to come to terms with what has happened. An assistant luggage clerk with Western Railway at Bombay Central, Rammilan got the job on compassionate grounds after the death of his father, Brijlal, three decades ago. He couldn't join work immediately as he was too young then. But when he did begin working in 1993, he started off like his father as a gang-man. Born and brought up in Murrani village of Pratapgarh district in Uttar Pradesh, Rammilan completed his higher secondary from the Gandhi Inter College. Working as a gang-man did not appeal to him. And so he sat for departmental tests and ultimately qualified to become an assistant luggage clerk. He was well known in his neighbourhood for hosting the birthdays of local kids in his house, and when the neighbourhood was getting a water connection he agreed to have the tap fixed outside his door.

Yogesh Doshi

Loved the simple ambience of hill stations

It was when she was preparing for her standard X exams, due in less than five months after the blasts, that 15-year-old Priyanka missed her father the most. 'Papa would make my time-table, schedule revisions, solve difficult problems, and even test me once I was ready,' she recalls. But Priyanka is mature enough to realize that she's on her own now. And that she has to give her life her best. 'He never pressured me,' she says. All Yogesh (42) wanted was to give Priyanka's 'first career milestone' the importance it deserved. And so, conversations at the dinner table would often revolve around the coming exams. A diamond broker, Yogesh set up his own business, Suraaj Diamonds, 15 years ago – soon after he cleared high school. 'More than engaging himself with further studies, he wanted to start a career,' says his elder brother Mukesh. Priyanka wants a career too, but not in diamond brokering. 'I want to study jewellery design,' she says with an air of finality. These days, she is also trying to spend more time with her 11-year-old sister, Binjal. Yogesh loved travelling. In fact, this Diwali, the family had planned to go to Tirupati. 'We were also planning a trip to the US,' says wife Shalini. But they decided against it because of Priyanka's exams. 'We didn't want her to be distracted,' she explains. Short holidays kept Yogesh going. It was just on Monday, the day before 7/11, that the family had returned from a three-day vacation to Lonavala. 'Lonavala was Yogesh's favourite weekend getaway. He loved the hill station's simple ambience,' says Shalini.

SHYAM SUNDER SHARMA

The King of Comedy

For comedian Shyam Sunder Sharma (54), his family was his last audience. 'Before leaving home on 7/11 he said: "I have switched many businesses, from selling tomatoes to starting a milk shop. At all times, my family members were the first to stand in queue rather than any customers."' That's how daughter Pratibha recalls the last time the Sharmas shared a laugh together. Shyam made people laugh and he loved being able to do so. They called him 'Jwalamukhi' or 'King of Comedy'. A 1987 Narayan Shankar Dixit awardee, Shyam had been the star of many a television show on SAB TV, Zee TV and Doordarshan. 'He was a class apart,' says younger son Rajesh as he brings out some of his father's trophies from the cupboard. 'We were so proud of him when his solo cassettes were released and his poems published in various magazines.' If Rajesh and Pratibha talk about his sense of humour, Shyam's widow, Shraddha Devi, also remembers him for his culinary skills. Suddenly, out of the blue, he would walk into the kitchen and start to prepare a dish. Later, as the family would sit down to eat, he would keep asking whether it was good. 'Most of the time, it was wonderful,' she recalls. Ever since he was a child growing up in Bhilwara in Rajasthan, Shyam wanted to write couplets, poems and jokes. More so, he was confident he could make a living out of it. So, even though he dabbled in several businesses – from selling tomatoes in wholesale to distributing milk – his mind was stuck on being a comedian. For the Sharmas, life will never be the same again. Yet, they believe, the show must go on.

GOVINDRAMJI DAVE

Was looking for a groom for his daughter

Two years ago, when Govindramji (54) became a grandfather, he decided to take it easy at work so that he could spend more time with his grandson. And so, after 17 years of dedicated service at a garment export firm in Santa Cruz, he started to come home earlier than usual. That meant he had become a regular on the 5.36 pm Borivali Local, which he would board at 6.08 pm at Santa Cruz. On 7/11, he was coming home as usual, when a blast on the train at Jogeshwari injured him seriously. He died in hospital. Born in Desuri village in Rajasthan, Govindramji was introduced to Bombay when he was a young boy in standard III. He ended up spending most of his early years in Juhu, where his father worked as a priest in a local temple. After finishing school, he did odd jobs until he landed the job in Santa Cruz. It had been a long struggle, but for once life for the Daves was finally looking up. Son, Hitesh, who studied in a corporation school, is today a CA and happily married, Kavita is doing her M.Com, Varsha has cleared standard X and youngest son Jitendra is still in school. The double income of father and son was helping all of them. 'We were finally seeing good days,' says wife Indiradevi. 'But now, he has left us.' If there was anything Govindramji disliked, it was visiting the hospital. 'He never liked hospitals. He would visit one only if it involved a close relative,' recalls daughter Varsha. That Tuesday, as they wheeled their father into Cooper hospital, he was still conscious. He told the doctors his full name, address and telephone number. But, sadly, he succumbed to his injuries soon after.

187 MUMBAI LIFE STORIES

Mohanan Thekkekara

Railwayman, wrote names of wife, son on his shirt with blood

Wife Gayathri couldn't find his name in the list of the injured. She identified him later, among the bodies, as he had scrawled her name and that of his son, on his shirt, with blood. Mohanan (41) worked with Western Railway as a senior estimator. He would usually return home around 8 pm but that day, he was on a train much earlier. There was an explosion in the train around 6.30 pm at Mira Road station and he was grievously hurt. He later succumbed to his injuries at the Bhakti Vedanta hospital. No one in the family will ever know why he was in the first class compartment of that train at that time. 'I still find it hard to believe he is not there any more,' says Gayathri, an investment consultant, who was married to Mohanan 14 years ago. Originally from Vellinazhi in Kerala, Mohanan was a civil engineer and had been with the railways since 1987. It was during the early years in the job that he and Gayathri worked in the same office and he proposed to her. 'We were the opposite of each other in nature, and in looks,' says Gayathri, admitting she didn't want to say no to the handsome man. Lately Gayathri has been spending a lot of time with her sons, Pranav, who is in class VII and Rahul a class V student. Rahul is too young to fully grasp the enormity of what has happened to the family. He was very close to his father and still thinks Mohanan will come back. Pranav is mature beyond his 13 years. 'Dad was a friend to me. When he had to tell me something he would do so in a manner I didn't feel bad about,' he says. 'He was my idol and kept our family happy.'

187 MUMBAI LIFE STORIES

Mahendra Motilal Mehta

Retired lawyer and company secretary, aspired to do a PhD

At 79, Mahendra Motilal Mehta felt he still had a lot to explore and learn. After working as a legal executive and company secretary for over four decades, he was eager to do what many young students of today might be overwhelmed by – a doctorate in Philosophy. In fact, he had enrolled for a PhD in Hinduism at the University of Mumbai. Classes were to begin on July 15 but the bomb blast at Jogeshwari four days before that cut short everything. 'He was not just physically fit but had a very active mind. Earlier this year, during exams for another course he was doing, he would get up at 4 am to study, something which my son Jeet did not do even during his board exams,' says Mahendra's petite daughter-in-law, Bela. Mehta's day would begin early. He would go through four dailies – three English and one Gujarati – have his meals at fixed times of the day and in the evening walk to a Brahmkumari ashram, a kilometre away, for his daily discussion on spiritual matters. He had also enrolled himself in a year-long certificate course in Vallabh Vedant Vaishnavism from the department of Philosophy, University of Mumbai in 2005. He got his first job as a lawyer with Scindia Steamship and Navigation Co. and later moved to Maniklal Kher Co. It was at Kamani Metals and Alloys Limited that he had his longest innings, of over three decades, as a legal executive and company secretary. Because of his willingness to help others with his knowledge, he was fondly called 'vakilji' in the neighbourhood.

Rajendra R. Dilloud

Railway contractor, loved to wear gold jewellery

Two thick gold chains with lockets, an ornate bracelet and four finger-rings – Rajendra R. Dilloud (45) wore enough gold to be mistaken for a popular music director. Immensely fond of his jewellery, Dilloud would have been wearing gold worth nearly Rs 5 lakh when he died in the serial blasts of July 11, while he was heading home from work. That night, when his family was handed over his body at the hospital, there was no sign of the jewellery on his body. 'Even the Rs 60,000 he was carrying to give his friend was missing,' says Dilloud's wife Darshanadevi. Ironically, whenever people would advise Dilloud not to wear so much gold as to attract the attention of thieves, he would say with his trademark humble smile: 'Let them steal my gold, it's not more precious than my life.' Dilloud also loved animals. In his Bhayander flat, there is a big aquarium occupying pride of place, as well as white rabbits and even a turtle in the living room. A father of three children – Mahendra, 20, Hemlata, 18, and younger son Devendra, 13 – Dilloud was a contractor for the railways and also owned a business in Borivali. His daughter Hemlata has applied for the job the railways has offered as compensation. But Darshanadevi is uncertain if she should take it, even though other options are drying up. 'How can a girl born and brought up in a well-to-do family work as a Group D staffer? The Western Railway should think about that.' Dilloud was a very religious man.'It's not God, but these terrorists who have written our fate. They destroyed our happy home,' says Darshanadevi bitterly. 'They should be hanged.'

Ninad Mahale

Deeply religious, yet a liberal

'*Hamari life banake, woh khud hi chale gaye,*' says Preeti about her brother-in-law, Ninad Mahale. For, it was he who had played a crucial role in convincing her conservative family to agree to her marriage with his younger brother-in-law, Sunil. 'Preeti and I wouldn't have been married had it not been for Ninad,' admits Sunil, who tied the knot with his long-time sweetheart less than a week before the 7/11 blasts killed him. 'We are from a very conservative Maharashtrian family and our parents couldn't fathom a love match,' explains Sunil, who runs a travel & tours business. It was Ninad's patient persuasion and gentle coaxing that finally led to the parents giving in. The Mahales moved into their modest Malad home two years back. And since it was close to wife Nita's maternal home too, it was easy for the two families to bond. 'He was like my son,' says Nita's mother Chandrika, 'and never a son-in-law with whom we had to be formal with.' Sunil adds that he was less a 'jeeja' and more a friend in whom they would all confide. A staunch Ganesh devotee, that Tuesday Ninad did what he did every Tuesday. He visited the Siddhivinayak Temple early in the morning for prayers and then went to work – he was an accounts manager at the Insurance and Reinsurance Consultancy, Sewri. And since he would be fasting throughout the day, he would return home earlier than usual to break his fast in the company of his family, primarily wife Nita. That day he was coming home to Malad having boarded the train at Parel. The 6.26 pm Mahim blast killed him.

MOHAN KENSALI

Son got off the train before the blast

Son Mayur was travelling first class on his way to Vasai from Borivali. Immediately after he stepped out of Mira Road station, there was a blast on the train. He survived only because he had got off to avoid the evening rush. But Mohan Kensali (43), wasn't that lucky. On the evening of 7/11 he was travelling in another local and died in the Borivali blast. A senior clerk with the income-tax department at Churchgate, Mohan would usually be back home around 9 pm. That day, he left early as father and son had planned to go shopping – Mayur was to join a hotel management course in Khandala the following week; a plan he has now dropped because of financial constraints. When Mayur saw his father's name on TV, he started working the phones and managed to get in touch with relatives. They rushed to Bhagwati hospital in Borivali where late at night, they were able to identify Mohan's body. It was taken to Mohan's younger brother, Naveen's place in Vile Parle and brought home in Vasai the next day for the funeral. 'Mohan was always fun to be with and we got along well,' recollects Naveen. 'Dad was a simple man and helpful in nature,' adds Mayur. 'Even the staff at our printing press loved and respected him, not only because he was their employer, but also because of his humanity.' Everyone agrees that Mohan was a hard-working man. And a testimony to that is his company 'Mayur Print' , which he set up himself and which today is one of Vasai's more popular printing presses.

SANJAY JASWANI

A home-bird, he loved spending time with the family

Sanjay Jaswani (38) travelled first class on Mumbai locals. But he would often give up his seat to a fellow commuter. 'His reasoning was that while people pay to travel first class, he had the privilege of travelling free,' says mother Rekha proudly about her son's railway credentials. As a section engineer with Western Railway's electrical department at Churchgate, Sanjay was loved and respected by all for his work ethic and sensitive nature. On 7/11, says another section engineer, Vishal Pawar, he was filling in for him. 'I had to leave early as my daughter was in hospital. But, he readily agreed to take over my workload.' That's how Sanjay will always be remembered. The eldest son of Mohan and Rekha Jaswani – both are retired railway employees – Sanjay was easy to get along with. 'He had a clean heart and would never hurt anyone intentionally. He never lost his temper either,' says Mohan. Sanjay was born in Ulhasnagar at a place that's still referred to as Camp Number 2. At work, Sanjay played a key role. Section engineer Mahendra Ghaisas recalls how he proved his worth as a sub-station engineer when he was entrusted with the responsibility of ensuring uninterrupted power supply for trains. 'He always maintained a positive attitude towards work,' says Ghaisas, a friend of his from their training days in Ajmer. 'He would execute his work diligently leaving no room for complaints.' Sanjay was a home-bird. He loved spending time with his family – parents, wife Vanita and son Kunal. And since Vanita also worked, he loved to stay at home during weekends doing odd jobs around the house or helping Kunal with his studies and project work.

Anuj Killawala

Insurance agent, daughter now looks after the business

It took the Killawalas a year-and-a-half to finally move into their well-furnished dream home in Vile Parle. Anuj Killawala (47) had just repaid their July dues of Rs 1 lakh and his family was counting the months when they would be paying the last instalment of their home loan. But the hard-working insurance man couldn't complete what he had started, his life rudely cut short by the 7/11 train blasts. 'He made our Aashiyana and when the time came to enjoy the fruits together, he left us,' says his widow Chandrika. The idea was to clear the loan as quickly as possible. And even though that meant a meagre bank balance, they were sure that as a successful development officer with the New India Insurance Company, Anuj would take care of the future. For the company, Anuj was an asset. He never wore a watch to work, lest he be distracted. 'He was a workaholic,' says 18-year-old daughter Kruti, who is now looking after her father's clients. 'He was a true marketing man, he would get the best deal for his clients.' These days, Kruti goes to office around 9 am and sits with her father's colleagues to understand the nature of his work and take part in 'strategy sessions'. Balancing work and time with college to pursue a B.Com degree is difficult. But Kruti is determined to make it work. 'Dad once asked an astrologer, "After my retirement, what will happen to the empire that I have built?" That time, I didn't quite understand what his "empire" was, after all, he was working for a government company,' she admits. 'Now I do. I see what he has left behind, and promise him, wherever he is, that I will not let his "empire" crumble.'

Parag Karambelkar

A Pharma consultant, who loved art, especially Amrita Sher-gil

Parag (53) was in the habit of writing a daily journal. Not at night before going to bed, but one that he updated when he did something or met someone significant. That's why it's important for his family, most of all daughter, Amruta, to find the missing suitcase in which he carried his diary. All they know is that he must have been returning home in Malad (West) from some official work in Panvel – he was a pharma consultant – when he was killed in the Mahim train blast. 'We are still looking for his briefcase. *Papa se kucch bhi baat nahi hua... Agar diary mil jaaye to pata to chalege Papa ne us din kya kya kiya,*' says Amruta, who describes her father as a 'time clock'. For she had never had to call him to ask: Where are you? Or, What are you doing? 'Dad had a fixed time for everything. He drank his juice at 8 am, ate dinner at 9 pm, took an evening walk at 9:30 pm. He detested wasting a second,' says Amruta, now pursuing an MA in Psychology. 'And he would update his diary throughout the day and read at night,' she recalls. 'He said it taught him time management. Also, it helped him introspect.' Parag, says his family, was a passionate man – passionate about life itself. 'He loved art and culture,' says Amruta, pointing to a colourful bookshelf with his collection of over 2000 books on painting, literature and music. No wonder he named his only daughter Amruta – after his favourite painter Amrita Sher-gil. 'We recently visited a Picasso exhibition. Dad would insist I spend my pocket money on books on art and culture,' she says.

Kalubhai Laxman Kasodariya

An avid swimmer and practitioner of yoga

His work in the diamond business always kept him busy. But during the months before he died, Kalubhai Laxman Kasodariya (42) was more occupied finalizing arrangements for his daughter's wedding fixed for February next year. 'He was very happy for me,' says his 20-year-old daughter Asha, who's studying for a commerce degree. 'He would constantly advise me on how to lead my life after marriage. He was really looking forward to it.' Kalubhai died on July 11. He usually returned home to Borivali only around 9 pm. But that Tuesday was Guru Purnima and he wanted to attend a satsang in the neighbourhood. So he left office early and took a train from Charni Road. The bomb went off in the first class compartment when the train reached Mahim station. Asha says Kalubhai – an avid swimmer and yoga practitioner – was very popular among his friends. They often tell the family that he 'was a very jovial person and cracked a lot of jokes'. His son Ketan is now learning his trade. Ketan says Kalubhai always wanted him to do that some day. 'I will run the business and study at the same time. But I miss him. Working together would have been different,' says Ketan. Financially, the Kasodariyas have been okay; they live in a joint family. But Kalubhai's wife Madhuben has gone into a shell. 'We were happy with whatever we had, but his death is painful,' says Asha. 'I shared all my secrets with my father. Whatever he decided for me was always perfect and I loved him a lot for that,' she says. '*Mujhe jitna pyaar mila mere Papa se, utna kisi ko nahi mila hoga.*'

187 MUMBAI LIFE STORIES

Vrindesh Seksaria

The popular boy next door

Ask anyone who knew him, and they'd say only one thing about Vrindesh Seksaria (23): he wanted to do something; become someone. Be it volleyball or organizing a community function, whatever he did, he did with pride and enthusiasm. So much so that his zeal would almost always rub off on others. Naturally, as parents of a very popular boy-next-door, the Seksarias were proud of their son. Even at such a young age, he had shown the ability to rally people around. His mother Radha refers to him as a Pied Piper. 'Vrindesh loved organizing programmes on festivals throughout the year. I remember the rain dance he did during Holi, which was a particular success – everyone followed him with their hearts.' A B.Com graduate, Vrindesh ultimately found himself in the diamond industry. Coming from an engineering background, it was difficult for his father, Ramanarayan Seksaria, to understand his son's choice of profession. Both father and son had had long discussions on this, but in the end his father gave in. 'Although they had their share of arguments,' recalls Radha, 'Vrindesh was a very obedient boy and never crossed the line. He knew his father spoke merely out of concern.' The only thing Vrindesh was fussy about was food. 'He didn't like junk food and unlike his friends in college, he would always come home for meals instead of eating outside,' she says. 'He was a finicky eater and picked one or two dishes out of all that was cooked at home.' For the Seksarias, trying to overcome a tragedy they were never ready to face is an arduous task. They are now distributing prayer books with anti-terror messages to their satsang group.

Rimanya Thakare

A bank peon, wife has taken up job of cleaning trains

Rimanya (35) would often tell his wife that if something should happen to him, she should sell their Vasai home and take their son Nikhil and settle down with her parents in Dadra and Nagar Haveli. 'Whenever he told me something like that, I used to get up and stomp out of the room,' says Nirmala. 'He would then come over and calm me down.' The truth was, she admits, that she could never imagine a life without her 'biggest strength'. Now, more than three months after 7/11, Nirmala is struggling to come to terms with her husband's death. More overwhelming is the challenge of survival. The immediate problem is to take care of the home loan instalments. Rimanya, who was a peon with the Citizen Credit Bank in Colaba, had got his sanctioned from there for their Vasai home when they moved in three years ago. Nirmala has already taken up the job offered by the railways. 'I work at Mumbai Central, where I have to clean the outstation trains that halt there.' But her greatest concern is for four-year-old Nikhil's future. 'It was Rimanya's decision to educate our son in an English medium school,' she says. 'Now, I am worried whether I'll be able to fulfil his wish.' Yes, finances are the problem. Already, she says, her in-laws are making life difficult after the compensation money came in. 'My father-in-law has asked for the money. He says Rimanya was his son and the money should go to him.' Ironically, it was Nirmala who had forced Rimanya to travel first class. 'I wanted him to be comfortable, so I forced him to take a first class season ticket and assured him we would manage by cutting down on some other expense,' she says.

BRIJMOHAN PRASAD

An insurance agent, his baby boy awaits another heart surgery

Wife Sunita hates cooking these days. For most of her memories of her husband are associated with food. The only thing that calmed his temperamental mood was food. If it had been a bad day, and he was upset, he could be brought around with paneer garnished with coriander. At other times, the two would simply eat out at the city's most fancy restaurants. 'Food was his only weakness,' recalls Sunita. 'And I knew how to use it. If the food didn't taste good, he would argue till his last breath saying, "Can't you make good food, you know I hate bad tasting food after a day's work,"' she mimics him and smiles. These are her memories. And these days, she lives by them. Sunita admits she was a strict vegetarian before her marriage. But it was Brijmohan's love for chicken and fish curry that made her lose her inhibitions. 'I started cooking chicken in our kitchen for him. You can say, he made me break the rule of my life. But I did it for him,' she adds. Born and brought up in Mumbai, Prasad(32) worked as an insurance agent with Max New York Life in Dadar, where colleagues remember him as a helpful person. 'He was like an agony aunt to all. In fact, many people used to approach him when they were scouting for a job and he would always help by pushing that person's case, especially if he was talented,' says Sunita. Now, Sunita's major worry is their five-month-old son Aijush's health. He was born with a hole in his heart. He recently underwent a major surgery at Holy Family hospital in Bandra for which they spent Rs 4 lakh. Now, she doesn't know how she will fund his future operations.

Jitendra Nagar

Had started taking the train after a recent bike mishap

A month before 7/11, a minor motorbike accident prompted Jitendra Nagar (52) to switch to trains. Today, nearly four months after he died in the serial train blasts, his widow Sangita can only blame destiny for what has happened. 'All memories associated with him are pleasant. How can anyone forget such a good person,' she says about her husband of over 30 years, describing him as a 'very good natured and humorous person'. He was also kind and went out of his way to help people. Jitendra, who worked for Hafincons Infotech and Industrial Services as a site manager at the Taj's Land's End hotel in Bandra, was adored by friends and colleagues. His son, Ashish, is also a mechanical engineer like his father and works with the Taj President at Colaba. 'After his death an eerie silence has enveloped the house. He was more like a friend to me,' says Ashish. Sangita will always remember her husband as a man who loved people. 'In gatherings, he wouldn't hesitate to accost familiar faces and introduce himself afresh just to have a conversation,' she recalls. Also, even though both her husband and son were in the hotel industry, they loved home food. 'Jitendra loved hot and spicy food and after work he would make sure he'd come home and have dinner with the family.' His colleagues too enjoyed his company. He was down-to-earth and never let office designations and hierarchy come in the way of making friends or doing something like having a meal with junior colleagues. 'He was a genuine *hasmukh*,' his friends all say.

Ramesh Nijai

A village schoolmaster, who loved to play the drums

The children of Borivali's Sur Vidhyalay miss their master. As does Kalamb Gaon, a village eight kilometres from Vasai where he was born. A restless soul, who loved to live life and face whatever challenges were thrown at him, Ramesh (42) was quite unlike any other village schoolmaster who taught Marathi. He had a flair for music. And though he could play almost anything – keyboard, harmonium, tabla – drums were his passion. 'Give any musical instrument to him and he'd play it to its best,' says Ramesh's cousin Ulkesh. At school, he had begun giving drumming lessons much to the delight of the children. All that came to a sudden halt on 7/11. Ramesh died in the Bhayander blast on his way home. Among his five siblings, Ramesh was the only one who pursued academics. 'He completed his B.Ed whereas I dropped out from school in class VIII. He had the zeal to study, which we all lacked,' admits Jayendra, who works as a peon in a private firm in Borivali. Ramesh was a hard-working man. His day would begin at 5 and end at midnight. He would start by helping Jayendra at their farm. 'Even after returning from school, Ramesh would visit our farm once.' The Nijai's are a family of modest means and Ramesh's job as primary schoolteacher meant a lot to them as the income from their farm was limited. It was after Ramesh got his school job that the family was assured of a steady income. Things had only just begun to look up. Ramesh had recently renovated his house and constructed a new floor to make extra room for his children.

Dilip Kashinath Kamath

LIC officer, loved dramas and documentary films

Dilip Kashinath Kamath (57) had begun planning for his retirement. Unhappy with the hectic pace of his life in Mumbai, he had almost made up his mind to move to a 'peaceful place' where he would have a farmhouse. Having spent his life insuring other people's lives, he thought, he would do something different: like social service or tuitions. Friends and colleagues knew Dilip as a knowledgeable person who was in love with movies and music. Since documentary films were the closest to his heart, he even took the initiative to launch a film society – *Kalachitra Mandal*– which he eventually registered in 1984 in Borivali. Among the friends who helped him set up the society is Pramod Korgaonkar, who knew him from his school days. 'I was highly influenced by his love for documentary movies and dramas. Ours was the first film society that existed between Dadar and Borivali in those days. We helped him, but it was his passion that kept the mandal alive for three years.' Daughter Shama can guess why his friends and colleagues thought him 'knowledgeable'. He was a voracious reader, she says. 'Talking to him was like learning something new everyday. He allowed me to do everything and never held me back because I was a girl.' Now, seated amid her father's vast collection of music cassettes, CDs and books, Shama is trying her best to come to terms with the hard reality of spending the rest of her life without her mentor. 'I am worried about the future as I have to play the role of father as well as mother,' says his wife Shailaja with remarkable composure.

Govind Solanki

Peon at BMC, never said no to anyone

Govind Solanki (42) could never say no for anything to anyone. That won him many admirers, but that's also the only thing about his father that Mahesh didn't like. 'It's nice to be kind to others but my father would go out of his way to bring a smile to someone's face. Often, we felt that people exploited him. We got angry on several occasions when he gave up his plans for someone else's work,' says Mahesh with a wry smile. Solanki worked as a peon for the Brihanmumbai Municipal Corporation (BMC). He was popular at office and at the housing society where he lived in Bhayander. Residents had made him their chairman. 'My father would organize everything – from garba during Navaratri to Diwali melas,' says Mahesh, eldest of his three sons. At office, Solanki's colleagues called him 'Tilakdhari' – a devotee of Chamunda Devi, he would never leave home without a tilak on his forehead. 'They always told us, "Your father and his tilak are inseparable,"' says Mahesh, who's now working in the municipal corporation. Solanki was a home-bird, and he loved to cook for his children. 'Often, he treated us to Gujarati sweets,' says Mahesh. 'On my last birthday, he made paneer bhaji, bhajia pau, baigan ka bharta and what not. We got the birthday cake from outside, but he spent hours decorating it with cream and we fought over who would eat the cherry.' Mahesh has preserved his father's wallet, which was found at the blast site. Inside, there's a bloodstained two-rupee note. 'No money on this earth is worth more than this for me,' says Mahesh as he wipes away his tears.

187 MUMBAI LIFE STORIES

Gokul Sharma

An electrical engineer, he didn't want to retire

Youngest of three siblings, Ajay decided to celebrate his July 13 birthday with the family. Most of all, he wanted to surprise his father, Gokul Sharma (62), and so he decided to take a few days off from running his own business to come down to Mumbai from Nagpur. He did, only to find to his horror that his father was one of those who had died in the July 11 serial train blasts. 'I guess, it was never meant to be,' says Ajay. 'What's more painful is that within three months we have lost two more members of our family, Gokul's parents,' says his widow Usha. 'The void he leaves behind can never be filled.' These days, the Sharmas find solace in their memories: Gokul's love for sweets, his restless nature that prevented him from idling at home, and his habit of writing down little notes on the day's events, however small, however nondescript. 'Everything in this house reminds us of him,' says Usha, who likes to describe her husband as a workaholic. The word, 'retirement' did not exist in his dictionary, she adds. An electrical engineer by qualification, he was an executive officer at the Cuffe Parade head office of Harinagar Sugar Mills. He'd been with them for 40 years. 'He was passionate about his work and worked seven days a week, even if it was Holi or Diwali,' says Usha. At the same time, his family ties were strong. 'He never forgot to call his eldest daughter Seema before leaving for office,' recalls his wife. Even now, daughter Seema, who stays with her husband in Udaipur, is yet to come to terms with her loss.

Ravindranath Banliharia

Hotel manager, was excited about new assignment in Daman

Ravindranath (42) was excited about his transfer to Daman where he would be in charge of a new hotel. And if everything went according to plan, his wife Vimla and their two children were to join him soon. But things did not happen as they had hoped. Ravindranath was among the 187 who died in the serial blasts on the packed local trains. The second of four siblings, Ravindranath was a pillar of strength for the family. His eldest brother is in the army, while the youngest, Virendra, is in Mumbai. Virendra is eternally grateful for what his bhai did to help him find a foothold in this city of dreams. 'He is the one who gave me tremendous support during my early days of struggle,' he says. Virendra, who is married with a son, now promises to do his bit. He says he will not leave his sister-in-law Vimla and Ravindranath's children but live with them in their Virar home – Ravindranath had bought the flat 12 years ago. 'Virendra will stay with bhabi and the children. He says he won't leave them at a time when they require his support the most,' confirms Narendra, brother No 3. That Narendra's Mumbai dream worked out, also has a lot to do with Ravindranath. 'He asked me to come here (from Himachal) and I did. He said Mumbai had better job prospects,' Narendra recalls. 'In fact, he even told me that if I didn't want to work I could stay in his house without feeling guilty.' But there wasn't any opportunity for that. Ravindranath had already spoken to a friend who recruited Narendra and gave him his first job in Mumbai.

Narottam Meher

In office, he disbursed salaries; everyone came for his funeral

The sprawling Meher family bungalow in the scenic village of Kalam in Nallasopara looks empty. His daughter Sneha, who is on extended leave from her job, answers the door. His wife Meeta has also not gone to work for the past four months. The silence in the house is overwhelming. 'I am very worried about my mother. She cannot bring herself to step out of the house. I hope by next month she feels better,' says Sneha, who works for Vodafone. The Mehers are yet to come to terms with their loss – Narottam Meher (53) died in the train blast at Meera Road while returning from the Pest Control of India, his workplace of 27 years. Narottam was a family man liked and loved by one and all. He would always worry about his children: Archana (25), Sneha (24), Jatin (22) and Kunal(17). 'Even if we were ten minutes late, he'd worry about us and get worked up. *Woh hamari rah dekhte the, ab hum unki rah dekhte hain,*' says Sneha. Narottam was passionate about food. 'My father loved eating fish. Every Sunday he would go to the market, select the right kind of fish and ask Mother to cook it for him,' she recalls. 'Even on his way home from work, he would often stop by in the market and buy some food stuff.' Narottam's job at the office was such that he came into contact with everybody. As administrative manager in PCI, he had to disburse the salaries of all the employees. 'The whole office was here during his funeral,' says Sneha. 'A lot of peons were crying. They said he was always very kind to them.'

MOHAMMED JAVED SHAIKH

Railway engineer, was waiting for his son's wedding

The family of Mohammed Javed Shaikh (52) lives in congested Naupada, Bandra (East) with one end of their tiny home overlooking the railway tracks. And, at 6.24 pm on July 11, the womenfolk of this household watched in shock as mangled bodies and grievously injured commuters were carried away after a train compartment blew up just outside Bandra station. At 11.30 pm, after a tension-fraught evening, Zaki Shaikh discovered that his father was lying dead in the morgue at Sion hospital. A senior section engineer (mechanical department) with Central Railways, Javed had nearly a decade of service left. Belonging to Allahabad, the Shaikhs were in Jabalpur until his transfer ten years ago. Posted at Katni junction– this little town in Madhya Pradesh boasts of Indian Railways' biggest wagon repair centre, biggest diesel loco-shed and a large electric loco-shed – the Shaikhs had lived in a township along with thousands of other railway employees, where the atmosphere was always cosmopolitan. 'We may be Mohammedans,' says his wife Shaida, 'but he was friendly with everybody, never fought with anybody, and definitely never on the basis of religion. Ask anyone in this chawl or at his workplace. His namaaz and his work, that is all he cared about,' she says, adding, 'Can any assistance replace my husband and what he meant to his family?'

Sandeep Bhonsle

A gentle, genuine person who adored his three little girls

A middle-aged Sikh lady answers the door to Sandeep Bhonsle's second floor apartment in Virar. She breaks into a warm smile while explaining that this is indeed the house of the 34-year-old Hyundai executive who lost his life in the Matunga blast. 'I am his mother-in-law, people get confused since he was a Maratha Hindu and we are Sikhs,' she says. As she rushes off to the kitchen to fetch water, she answers what she anticipates the next question will be: 'No, Mini and he did not have a love marriage. I chose Sandeep for my daughter for I saw what a gem of a man he was; I felt my daughter would be happy with him as well.' She fondly recollects how it took time to convince her daughter about the match. It is a few hours before Manjeet, or Mini as she is called at home, returns home exhausted from work and explains, 'I was very young; I complained that he was very dark and stout,' she pauses. 'But my brother and sister were so fond of him that I started going for outings with all of them. That is when I got to understand and really like him for being the gentle, genuine person he was. Then, before our own daughters were born, he suggested we adopt Gwenial. He adored our little girls,' says Manjeet. Every day Sandeep's return from office would be marked by much excitement and fun and games. 'All three girls would just clamber all over him, to see what gifts he had got for them in his briefcase. "Alladin ka chirag" I would call it,' Manjit says with a wistful smile. 'He loved to pamper us all. I cannot bear life without him.'

SANJAY SAMANT

Excise inspector, always wanted to donate his eyes

In 1999, Sanjay Samant (46) had decided he would donate his eyes after death. But, death on the rail-tracks on 7/11 meant that nobody looked in his wallet for his eye donor's card. And when his family did recover his body the next morning, it was too late. 'The eyes had to be removed within two hours of death,' explains wife Shweta as she smiles and recalls how, years ago, they had together pledged their eyes. Their three-year-old son, Sumit, dutifully brings out the blue donor's card, among the only remaining memories of his father from Terrible Tuesday. As on any other day for this Central Excise Inspector, Sanjay was heading home to Goregaon from his Dadar office. He died in the Bandra blast at 6.24 pm. Says Sanjay's sister Shambhavi, 'There were two anchors in his life. Work and family.' A commerce graduate from Patkar College, Goregaon, Sanjay had joined the Excise department almost two decades ago. And every day, after returning home around 7 pm, he would spend at least two hours with the children. 'He would begin by taking up our elder son Sanjit's studies every day and then playing chess or carrom with the kids, depending on their mood,' says Shweta. For Sanjit, who is nine, Sanjay was more of a friend. 'He would always confide in him, telling him about the smallest of incidents at school.' These days, explains Shweta, Sanjit misses his father's painstaking explanations about all that was happening in and around the city. 'He would read him important newspaper articles or tell him a story that was significant,' adds sister Shambhavi.

ZUBAIR PATHAN

Youngest in the family, came to Mumbai to become a CA

The room's kept locked but cleaned every day. Not even the bedspread has been changed. For everything, from the paint to the chandeliers, to the matching glass vase by his bedside, was personally picked by Zubair Pathan (20). Father Irtiza Pathan has decreed that his room shall remain this way forever. 'He was my friend, not my son,' says Irtiza about Zubair. Owner of an industrial unit manufacturing welding machines, he admits he loved to indulge his youngest child. '*Woh kabhi mayus hua nahin zindagi mein,* ' he adds. Irtiza liked that. So, the carefree Zubair would travel only by Rajdhani Express or by plane. And when he was home, his father never objected to the huge telephone bills he'd run up speaking to his friends. 'He would travel by air during school days. So, in Mumbai if it was the local trains, it had to be first class.' And if anyone chided him for his expensive habits, Zubair would mischievously tug at his father's beard and say: 'Dada Thakur, who else will spend the money?' Zubair spent most of his young life away from home. First in boarding school at Nainital and then in New Delhi. So when he wanted to go to Mumbai, they were reluctant to let him go. These days, Irtiza finds comfort in looking through Zubair's belongings in his room: his suits, his college textbooks, a soft toy he had bought for his nephew and kept in the wardrobe. He found a school book in which Zubair had written the name of his favourite teacher at Delhi's Hamdard School, Mrs Savita Khanna. That he hated science and did not have a favourite 'male teacher' found mention as a postscript.

187 MUMBAI LIFE STORIES

Prashant Bendale

Married for only 26 days

His '*Aai*' still rings in Manik Chaudhari's ears. As Prashant Bendale's mother-in-law, she feels it was a privilege to be called so by him. For Prashant (28) had quickly endeared himself to his in-laws. Her daughter Leena is still struggling to assimilate the news that her husband of 26 days is no more. On leave since mid-June, Prashant had resumed work the previous day, which was also the first day he'd travelled by train. Marriage meant that Prashant had to swap his bachelor pad at Bandra for a larger, rented place. And he didn't want to ride his motorcycle to work every day. So, he settled for the train. His wife Leena, an electronics and telecommunications engineer from Cummins College in Pune, can't believe he is no more. Since it was an arranged marriage, Leena was just getting to know the man she would be spending her life with. They'd got engaged in May and after the wedding on June 16 in Jalgaon had come back to Mumbai on July 9 to begin their lives together. Prashant was a deputy manager with Essar Shipping and would travel from their home in Goregaon to his office. 'He was the kindest and most considerate person I have met. That's why I married him.' Prashant, son of a village schoolteacher and homemaker from Lasalgaon near Nashik, had come up in life the hard way. A keen learner, for him a sound education was of utmost importance. After graduating from the Government College of Engineering (Pune), Prashant went on to pursue his MBA from the Symbiosis Institute in Pune.

187 MUMBAI LIFE STORIES

CHANDRASEN BANGDIWALA

Sharebroker, came from Surat in '54

Chandrasen Bangdiwala (72) came to Bombay from Surat in 1954 looking for a job. He joined the Stock Exchange. In the next few years, as a clerk at the Exchange, he learnt a thing or two about trading and moved on to join a private share-brokering firm in 1960. He was with them till he died on 7/11. Stability and consistency were his hallmark. As a sub-broker with Deepchand L. Taswala, that's what he represented when clients came with investments. 'He did not believe in taking undue risks,' says his brother, Gulabchand Surti. 'He operated within safety margins. Even his clients, who were people who didn't like risks, trusted him and stayed with him for decades.' Chandrasen never felt the need to adopt or adapt to every change that came his way. For instance, though stock trading has been computerized , he never learnt the new, online system. 'He came from a different environment and did not feel the need for it. Computers were handled by others,' says Gulabchand. Chandrasen's life was uncomplicated: 'After alighting at Malad station on his way home from work, he would buy vegetables which he cooked on his own. He didn't enjoy having food prepared by others,' recalls Gulabchand. Chandrasen was also known for his punctuality. He was always on time, commuting from his Malad home to the Bombay Stock Exchange and back. Chandrasen had come to Bombay as a bachelor and died a bachelor. Even in his last days, says Gulabchand, he had no regrets.

Hasan Siraj Patel

Was planning to go on Haj after retiring in December

The Vasai neighbourhood of Koliwada will always remember him for his terrace. That was where he would hold classes for children – not paid tuitions, but something the Maulana did for free became of his love for children. A deputy general manager of the Abhyudaya Cooperative Bank at Kurla, Hasan Siraj Patel (58) was to retire in December. And he had already made plans: to fulfil a long cherished dream of going on his maiden Haj. He would have, had it not been for the train blasts on 7/11. He died in the explosion on the Dadar–Vasi Local. Wife Shamshad Begum Patel is still struggling to come to terms with the tragedy. 'Mummy is very depressed as she cannot face the reality of his death,' says son Anjum, a computer operator with the Bombay Mercantile Bank at Masjid Bunder. Other than his deep commitment to do voluntary service at schools and orphanages, Hasan was completely devoted to his banking work. Known amongst colleagues as a team player, he helped in the establishment of the Vasai Mahila Utkarsh Sahakari Pathpedi Maryahid, a credit society for women, of which his wife is manager. Even today, the family discusses the cruel twist of fate that led Hasan to the ill-fated train. Usually, he would travel to his bank at Kurla from Bhayander in a company-provided car. He used the train to commute between Vasai and Bhayander. Unfortunately, on 7/11 his driver reported sick. So he had a colleague drop him to the Dadar station where he boarded a local to Vasai. It was to be his last journey.

Francis Lewis

Engineer with Voltas, was relieved his children were settled

In his one-bedroom flat on Navghar Road the silence is overwhelming. Francis Lewis's family has been living one day at a time for the past eight months since their 'pillar of support' disappeared from their lives. A project manager with Voltas, Francis (52) had to travel a lot within the city. His last assignment was to supervise the completion of the air-conditioning work at Deutsche Bank, Lower Parel. The rest of his time was for his family. 'In fact, we were his world,' recalls daughter Shaila. A fun-loving father, Francis's only worry was his children's future. He'd heaved a sigh of relief when son Joel – who took loans to complete his education – landed a job in a software company at Khar. Shaila, too, had her sights set on a career. A third-year B.Com student at St Andrews College in Bandra, she has completed an International Air Travel Association (IATA) course. For wife Prescilla, he was the perfect husband who 'loved to eat whatever I cooked' and a loving father to their children. 'He would discipline them with his love,' she says with a smile. Shaila talks of the time when she would refuse to wake up early to go to school but once she would see her father was up and about, she would promptly get ready. Though he rarely voiced it, Francis was looking forward to his retirement. 'He wanted to relax after his retirement, for he had slogged through his working life,' says Shaila. Prescilla's only consolation is that both children were well on their way to making a life for themselves during his lifetime. 'He always said, "I am happy that my kids are settled in their lives."'

187 MUMBAI LIFE STORIES

Mohammad Tahir Ansari

A young guardian to a large family

Three years ago when Mohammad Tahir Ansari (25), the eldest among three brothers and four sisters, came to Mumbai, he had only one dream: to provide for his family. His father was without a job, and he had four sisters who had to be married off. As a computer hardware engineer with Tata Indicom – his office was in Bandra – this eastern UP boy had only just begun to feel somewhat optimistic about life. Living with his uncle, he was finally able to put away some money on the side and the future didn't look that bleak after all. But 7/11 changed everything. Not many in his family want to talk about his demise. But the youngest among Tahir's siblings, Mohammad Shaquib, is devastated. 'My brother was my only friend. He used to play with me a lot when he was here in Kunda. We are totally shaken, we miss him a lot.' What's making it even more difficult for the family is that Tahir was engaged. Shahina, who lives in a labour settlement in Bandra, and he were to be married soon; that day, it was she who played a large part in looking for and finally finding him in hospital. Tahir's father and a brother are in Mumbai carrying his photographs and documents to prove his identity so that they can get the compensation. '*Paisa to kal khatam ho jayega, nahi khatam honge to uski yadein,*' says his heartbroken mother Salma, who lost her own father when she was 13. 'Whom should we complain to? The government takes action only after an incident happens. It never takes precautionary measures, so that the lives of hundreds of innocent breadwinners are not trifled with.'

Madhu Pawar

Businessman, came to Mumbai to give family a better life

After working hard for years, Madhu Pawar, at sixty, was finally slowing down: he had struggled all through to give his family all that they needed, but had found little time to spend with them. 'The blast on July 11 killed him and his plans,' says son Shodhan. Pawar grew up in Belgaum and wanted to become an engineer. 'He was a brilliant student. But my grandparents did not have even Rs 100 at that time,' says Shodhan. In his late twenties, Pawar shifted to Mumbai. He had to: three brothers and four sisters were looking to him for support. For five years he worked as a teacher. And then he changed his career. That happened after a chance meeting with his childhood friend Amar Metrani, who, incidentally, died ten days before the July 11 serial blasts. Together, they set up an adhesive tape manufacturing company, Tapex Corporation, in Belgaum. Pawar became its marketing manager in Mumbai. One thing that Pawar strongly believed in was that professional and personal lives should not be mixed. Consequently, his wife Shruti, daughter Kunali, and Shodhan knew little about his work. 'He worked hard just to give us and his brothers and sisters a decent life. Ironically, now that he is no more, some of them seem to have disappeared from our lives,' says Shruti. The family remembers Pawar's love for non-vegetarian food, books and music. 'He probably had all the records of Lata Mangeshkar. And he loved to read. He made it a point to read up on any issue before discussing it,' says Shodhan.

Tejas Shah

Sales manager with Dabur, was his family's source of strength

As a teenager, Tejas Shah (31) had never found time to do what other kids his age were doing. He had to start working part-time when he was in school: his father had epilepsy and couldn't find a steady job. Life was the same during his college years and thereafter. 'Tejas was our pillar,' says his mother Chandrakanta. Now, nearly five months after the serial blasts of July 11, younger brother Mihir is doing his best to provide for the family, running a wholesale business in groceries that Tejas had helped him set up. Tejas worked for Dabur India Limited as a senior sales manager. He started working when he was in standard XII. He would rush to school in the morning and after classes head straight for the cosmetics shop where he worked part-time as a sales boy. His father Chandrakant had also worked as a salesman in stores, selling medicines and groceries, but never for long at one place – he would become unwanted as soon as he had an epileptic fit. *'Apne bete ko maine papad bana bana kar paala hai. Mein papad ghar main banake dukaano main bechti thi,'* says mother Chandrakanta. She says the family's financial problems transformed Tejas into a very serious and responsible person. 'He never demanded anything from us …new clothes, good food...nothing. His only dream was to earn money and give his brother and parents a decent life.' At work, Tejas was liked and admired. 'Even now his seniors from office call me up to say they miss him. He was so hard-working and dependable,' says his mother.

Dilip Kirale

An HPCL employee, left work early for Guru Purnima

A senior accounts assistant with Hindustan Petroleum Corporation Ltd at Bandra, Dilip Kirale (50) was an ardent devotee of Sai Baba. That day, he was to visit the Shirdi Sai Baba temple and was therefore not on his usual train. 'He was a jolly person and used to spend a fair amount of time with our son Sourav,' his wife Vibhavari recalls. 'Together, they would often go out – watch movies, visit places.' And these days, though Sourav seems to have found comfort among friends, he is no more the happy child he was. But Vibhavari keeps coming back to 7/11. She can't fathom how a matter of a few seconds could bring about such catastrophe for her family. 'According to a colleague, Dilip would always travel in a first class compartment that was either in the middle or at the end of the train, but never in a compartment at the front of the train. However, that day he had boarded the first class compartment in front,' says Vibhavari. His brother Shankar and other relatives rushed to Kasturi hospital in Bhayander immediately when they heard of the accident. 'By 2 am, I started having doubts. What could have happened? How badly was he hurt? I began to think that something was terribly wrong,' recalls Vibhavari. Shankar identified his brother's body by his identity card. The rest of his belongings, a diamond ring, chain, credit card and some cash, were missing. Friends and family remember Dilip for his kindness. 'He did not bother about money and always used to go out of his way to help others,' says Vibhavari.

Dalpat Masekar

An intrepid traveller, adored by his colleagues

In the fifth floor office of the electrical department of Western Railway at Churchgate, July 11 is a painful memory. Three officers from the department died in the serial blasts that day. Dalpat Masekar (54) was one of them. He and two colleagues were returning home together when a bomb went off in their train at Khar station. All three died on the spot. 'We had tea at 4.30 pm. And after work, we left office together at 5.45 pm. Like on other days, I took the Virar Fast, he boarded the 5.54 Borivali Fast. Who would have thought something like this would happen?' says Anil Kantharia, typist to the office superintendent in the electrical department, still coming to terms with the loss of a friend and boss. Masekar came to Mumbai in 1980 for a career in the railways. He did well, and went on to head the electrical department in Western Railway's Churchgate office. Initially, he lived alone in Matunga. But after he moved up, the family shifted to the middle class locality of Ashok Van in Borivali East, near the Sanjay Gandhi National Park. 'He was very particular about work. He introduced a new system of maintaining files that we are still following. He never had a problem with anyone, but he would expect you to do your work efficiently,' recalls long-time colleague Shubhada Patade, office superintendent in the electrical department. 'That weekend we were planning to go to Lonavala with my uncle and aunt,' says son Saurabh. 'But it was not to be.' Saurabh misses his father, who always encouraged him. 'Even when I failed in the IXth standard, he supported me,' he says.

187 MUMBAI LIFE STORIES

Dr Girish Parmanand

Patients don't want his clinic to shut, so wife plans to run it

He was the archetypal gentle doctor, taking the local train every day for 40 years to reach his suburban clinic half an hour away, never slacking, even at age 71, and not once raising his voice during those decades of dedicated practice. 'A man with so much compassion,' said a young patient outside Dr Girish Parmanand's clinic at Goregaon (East), 'he didn't deserve such a brutal death.' Says son Amit, employed with a multinational bank and posted in Singapore, 'He was very dedicated to his practice. For him, his patients came first, everything else later. He would forgo even his own comfort for his practice.' That single-minded commitment may have sometimes irked wife Sulbha, a doctor herself. Still, his clinic is now drawing her back to Mumbai. With her son, daughter-in-law and grandchild since the tragedy, she's now planning to return home, to take over her husband's practice. Dr Parmanand was the 'typical' cricket fanatic, though he also loved watching soccer matches on television. Bollywood and the daily newspaper were the other staples. At their Khar residence, the building's cooperative housing society chairman, S.P. Bhatia, remembers his neighbour as a 'thorough gentleman'. Always soft-spoken, quietly cheerful, somewhat shy – neighbours barely knew the family member – he was rarely ever at home, spending long hours at his clinic. 'He lived here for so many decades,' says Bhatia, 'but there was not a single argument he was involved in.' The high ethical standards of the profession never daunted the general physician. 'He never indulged in any malpractice,' says Amit.

AMRAT PATEL

A government clerk, family will move to their new flat soon

His one wish was to own a home in Mumbai, and after his daughter Bhakti was born, this became a mission. He was six months away from achieving his goal when he died. Four months after Terrible Tuesday, his wife Radha and his daughter Bhakti comfort each other with the thought that they will be able to fulfil 45-year-old Amrat Patel's wish. 'His dream of shifting to a new house is the only thing we are now looking forward to,' Radha explains. And no, the past months haven't been easy. Bhakti is still traumatized. So much so, she sometimes wakes up in the middle of the night, crying. A class IV student she has withdrawn into herself and hardly talks to anyone. 'I miss Pappa. He was my best friend,' is all she can come up with. Bhakti, who was born 12 years after the Patels married, was always very close to her father, says Radha. 'Now, she is even reluctant to put a garland on his portrait on the wall since it signifies Amrat is no more.' That day, after finishing work around 5.30 pm as usual, Amrat boarded a local from Churchgate to go to Borivali. And, as always, he was travelling first class. The blast at Mahim killed him on the spot even though he was rushed to KEM hospital by one of Mumbai's Good Samaritans. For his wife and daughter back home, it was an agonizing wait, which began soon after 7.30 pm, the time he would usually be home. 'We did not get to know till the next day that he was one of the victims of the blasts,' recalls Radha. 'It was only after Amrat's elder brother visited the hospital that we learnt what had happened to him.'

K. Bhujang Shetty

Blessed with a son after Terrible Tuesday

Shlok will never know that his father was a jovial, ever-smiling man. For he was born 33 days after his father, K. Bhujang Shetty (42), died in the blasts of 7/11. But young Shreya knew her father well – as well as only an eight-year-old can. She believes if she prays hard enough, her dad will come back. Bhujang, or K.B. Shetty, as he was popularly known among friends and colleagues, was a structural consultant who had quit his job and was operating from their Kandivali home. Mostly out of the city on tours, it was unfortunate that he found himself on a train in Dadar to go to Bandra. 'For the past few years, he was operating from home. He was a complete family man,' recalls Sumangala. 'We used to spend a lot of time together whenever he was free.' Soon after Terrible Tuesday, Sumangala's family brought her to Pune, as she was in the last month of her pregnancy. Shreya was admitted to the St Joseph's School in Pashan and the family is trying desperately to start all over again. 'He was very attached to his daughter,' says Sumangala's mother Vasanthi. Shreya, she says, is no longer the bubbly and chirpy girl she used to be. 'She has become very quiet,' adds Sumangala. 'Sometimes she thinks praying hard will get her father back.' For Sumangala, the responsibility of bringing up two children is weighing on her. 'I have been a housewife for the past ten years. Now I will have to look for a job. My family is there but I still need to stand on my feet,' she says. But she knows she'll have the help and support of Bhujang's friends and colleagues, all of whom rushed to help them during the initial days after the accident.

Manuel D'Souza

Dreamt of solving rural India's water problems

Barely a month after 35-year-old Manuel D'Souza was killed in the July 11 serial blasts, his father passed away. 'He fell ill and lost interest in life after his son's death; they were very close,' says Manuel's brother-in-law, Prakash Almeida. 'God had chalked out Manuel's life and he lived it. Now, I will lead mine, taking care of the children,' says wife Sarla, who works as a librarian at Utpal Sanghvi School in Juhu. Sarla is trying to gather the pieces of her shattered life and look ahead. But it's been difficult. Family friend Amita Naik, who knew the couple for many years, says that Manuel and Sarla were 'made for each other'; and that Manuel was the kind of person who would easily win hearts – a sentiment echoed by his colleagues. A chemical engineer, Manuel's big dream was to solve the water problems of rural India. He worked for Super Flow, a water treatment firm in Worli as a senior sales engineer. 'He was a bright student and brilliant at his work,' says his brother-in-law, explaining why Manuel's boss had entrusted him with the responsibility of conducting seminars on water treatment in other countries. That day, Manuel was returning home to Nallasopara when a bomb went off just as the train reached Matunga station. Manuel died instantly. Six months before he died, Manuel had turned spiritual and had started reading the Upanishads and the biographies of saints. Sarla and the family say his passing is a 'spiritual challenge', and they have found solace in prayers. 'We will stand tall and fight it out,' they say.

ANIS SATTAR PATEL

Came to Mumbai from Jalgaon, loved plants and shayari

Anis Patel (43) loved to take care of his plants. His family also knew him to be a *shayar* – writing couplets on current affairs whenever an idea came to him. But four months after he died in the 7/11 blasts, they just can't get over his last verse: *Aaj kal jo beej boye jameen mein, ped pur ugte hain bomb hi.* 'He would write about things that were happening all around him. The house is filled with diaries containing his *shayari*,' says his uncle Nabba Patel. Having lost his father when he was a toddler, hard work is something Anis was used to. His early years were spent in his grandparents' house in Jalgaon with his mother and two older siblings. Later, the family moved to Mumbai in search of better prospects. Anis was a stickler for neatness. Everything in the house had to be in place. 'I would never have dared to sit here in the hall and clean bombil fish,' says his aunt reminiscently. 'He was very particular about keeping the house spic-and-span at all times. Now it is in disarray.' Days after his death, the family found a packet containing 1400 rupees – money they knew he had set aside from his monthly salary of 8000 rupees for a yearly donation during Ramzan. Most of Anis's Sundays were spent tending to the plants in the verandah. 'He was very fond of plants. He would take good care of them,' says Nabba, recalling how the moment he entered the house after work, he would go over and take a look at his plants. 'But now, for the last four months, no one has been looking after them and they have all withered away. The entire look of the house has changed.'

Amresh Sawant

Engineer with Siemens, was always good at sports

Wearing a sunny yellow T-shirt and a bright smile, Amresh's king-size photograph is now the centrepiece of the Sawants' modest living room in their Andheri residence. But before he was suddenly snatched away from them on 7/11, the youngest of their three children was undoubtedly the apple of their eyes. Around six feet tall, Amresh (25) was a super athlete and a keen sportsman – swimming and jogging were his favourites. 'I think he was in class IV when we moved from Bandra to Andheri. That's when we enrolled him for swimming classes at the Andheri Sports Complex,' recollects father Madhukar. Throughout his school days, Amresh kept the habit. And in college, he was an asset to the football team. 'He represented his college in several championships,' says mother Jayshree, as she brings out a photo album, proudly pointing to her son beaming after winning a contest, dressed in formals for a presentation ceremony, hanging out with friends on the campus. 'That's him in office with his laptop,' his father chips in. After finishing school from Paranjpe Vidyalaya in Andheri, Amresh moved to Ahmednagar to pursue his higher studies. He did his BE from the Sanjivani Education Engineering College in Kopargaon (Ahmednagar). 'He was not really into software, his forte was networking,' says Madhukar. Apart from his BE degree, Amresh had also completed two certificate courses – one offered by Microsoft and the other by Cisco – 'for value addition'. His colleagues in Siemens all miss him. 'Amresh was a hard-working and dedicated team member,' they say.

Cyrus Jehangir Munshi

Moved to new home two days before 7/11

They had shifted to their dream home two days before Terrible Tuesday. He had got himself a new job and since his life's investment in the new flat at Vasai had finally materialized, Cyrus (31) was thinking it would be a good time to permanently shift out from Chennai, where he was earlier based, with his wife and six-year-old son. His excitement knew no bounds. 'He was from a small village in Mandvi but had big dreams. And he always wanted to shift to a big city,' says his wife Farzin. 'We went to Chennai for a year, but did not like it there. It was our dream to shift to Mumbai where there were a lot more people from our community.' They did, and finally it looked as if things were falling into place for them, recalls Farzin, who had married Cyrus seven years ago. He had just joined his new workplace: Parikh Brothers in Churchgate. More than four months after 7/11, even though Farzin has been trying very hard to keep her mind off it, she can't stop thinking of Terrible Tuesday and how 'normal' everything was until the blasts in the evening. For Farzin, their dream came crashing on 7/11 when her husband died in a train blast. Today, she has shifted back to her hometown of Navsari with son Jehzan, who cries every night before he goes to sleep, since his father has 'stopped coming home'. And their dream flat? Farzin has had to sell it. 'I have sold the flat and put the money in a bank as security for my child's education. I plan to buy him a computer soon,' she says. After all, she has no choice but to move on.

Michael Dabre

A bank agent, his favourite movie was Anand

Gracy wishes she would feel better, sitting in her newly-built balcony – something which her husband Michael(51) had started but couldn't complete. How she wishes he was beside her admonishing her with his favourite line: 'Gracy, you know nothing about life!' But after 7/11, does anyone? 'I know he would be very happy that I have learnt to deal with people and was able to complete his unfulfilled dream,' says Gracy, as she talks about her husband of 17 years and his plans for the future. Michael was done with his commitments – helping his brothers build their homes, settling two of his sisters – and had decided to get on with his all-time wish of converting their Nallasopara bungalow into a duplex. He had taken a loan to start work and had planned the instalments in such a way that by December all dues would be repaid. 'He also promised me all worries will come to an end with Christmas,' recalls Gracy. But these days, she is bracing herself to spend Christmas without him. To her, Michael was the 'ultimate' family man, easy-going and happy, who enjoyed his evening whisky. 'My family has seen several deaths, but he was always there to hold us together,' she says with 15-year-old daughter Tejaswita beside her. Even though life had dealt many a cruel blow, he was brave enough to face them. His elder sister died the day before his wedding and his second sister, a nun, died in February. 'He would always recall the story of the Rajesh Khanna movie *Anand* (whose hero valiantly battles a terminal illness) and tell me to draw inspiration from it,' says Gracy. 'Now, I realize the meaning of it.'

Chandrakanth Mithani

An accountant, he was enjoying being a grandfather

On December 3 2005, Chandrakanth Mithani broke from his daily routine for the first time in 65 years: he left work mid-way. The reason was worth it. His daughter had given birth to a son. And so he picked up the largest bouquet he could find, boarded a local from Charni Road station and came rushing to Goregaon. Son-in-law Rupesh Sanghrajka believes Dhruv's birth was the only time he was so lavish, and that it was one of those rare occasions when he didn't hide his emotions. That evening, Chandrakanth, an accountant with a private firm at Charni Road earning Rs 10,000 per month, told his wife Malti that he had arrived; that all that he had wished for in life, was his. '"My struggle of the last forty years has paid off. Now I can rest in peace," he told me,' she recalls. A matriculate from Gujarat, Chandrakanth always had a fascination for numbers and accounting. 'While he used to do accounting at office, he taught me how to budget and save even with that small amount,' she says. 'Till date, I have never felt that I missed out on any of life's luxuries as he ensured that all material needs of the family, including that of his mother and our two daughters, were met.' Throughout his life, Chandrakanth loved Mumbai. 'Of late he had got tired of the commute,' says Rupesh. 'On his way back, he would come standing. For he thought he needed the exercise after spending the day sitting at his office desk. But, he never missed that fast train.'

ARVIND CHIKNE

The star of his village, he worked in a jewellery unit in Mumbai

It's at 6 am every day that Pandurang Chikne remembers his dead brother. In his tiny, attic-style home in a suburban slum in Mumbai, the first thought that strikes the school bus driver when he crawls out of bed is that he won't be tripping on his still-asleep brother's legs. 'He had long legs, *na*,' Pandurang says. Then, pointing to the trapdoor that serves as the entrance, he says: 'He'd be stretched out till there.' At 5 feet 7, 25-year-old Arvind was considered quite tall in their little village of Umbri in Taluka Poladpur, Raigad district. A champion cricketer with genuine swing when he bowled, Arvind had come to Mumbai dreaming of a job in the armed forces. His dream died after some failed attempts at army and navy physical endurance tests. A BA from Sunderrao More College of Arts and Commerce in Poladpur but unable to speak English, he found even his degree useless. Finally, he found an apprenticeship at a semi-precious jewellery manufacturing unit in Jogeshwari, staying at his workplace for a year while learning the trade. Four months before he died, he had shifted into his brother's home in Ghatkopar, to live with Pandurang, his wife Chhaya and two-year-old daughter, Mitali. In those four months, he maintained meticulous accounts on the back pages of an old notebook. In June, he'd actually saved most of his meagre earnings – Mitali was growing up, he had plans for the future. And though he pursued other Mumbai dreams for a year, those died too when a window bar from one of 7/11's ill-fated trains pierced his abdomen.

ANIL SATWANI

Senior railways clerk who loved sports and music

The last time Kajal Satwani spoke to her husband Anil (39) was when they met near the office lift around 5 pm on July 11. Employees with Western Railway, they both worked in the same building and usually returned home in the same train. But that day, he had called her down to say he was leaving early. It was Guru Purnima and he wanted to buy a present for his daughter's dance teacher. 'The day before, he had cooked for us. My children say the food tasted so good. How can I cook like him?' says Kajal, wiping her tears. Anil worked as a senior clerk in the pass section of Western Railway, which he had joined in 1989. Kajal is an assistant in the signals and telecommunications department. They fell in love 15 years ago and got married five years later. 'He was so jovial and caring. He would never say no to anyone,' says Kajal. 'He would have turned 40 on February 19 and we would have been married for 11 years on January 4.' Anil was fond of music and dance – a passion shared by his daughters, says Kajal. And he was also deeply involved in sports and cultural activities at work. Even on Sundays, he found time to play cricket with the children of his housing society. 'His level of energy surprised us,' says colleague Shanti Chandran. 'He was such a helpful person that even in the night he didn't hesitate to rush to someone's assistance,' reminisces his wife. 'Everybody he knew wept for him. It's difficult not to think about him all the time.'

MAQSOOD DARVESH

Auto insurance man, now wife teaches the Koran to young girls

Amiable and generous, Maqsood Darvesh (43) loved treating his friends to meals. An auto consultant and insurance advisor, his small shop outside the Regional Transport Office in Mahalaxmi was where a motley group of six would converge every afternoon for a gastronomic party. 'We only had to tell bhai what we wanted, and the steaming food would arrive in minutes,' smiles Ayub Khan, part of the group. Working at Shama Photo Studio next door, Ayub will always miss Maqsood enjoying his favourite Dabba Ghosht from the Grant Road Delhi Darbar restaurant. Post 7/11, Ayub is also trying to get used to the idea of a trip to Chowpatty or Haji Ali alone. They went there for evening walks together. Usually, Maqsood would take the 6:04 pm train from Mumbai Central accompanied by his Man Friday Moin Ansari, with him for six years, ever since he came to Mumbai from Jharkhand in search of a livelihood. These days, Maqsood's nephew Shoib supervises affairs at his shop. 'He does not come in every day, just once in a while,' says Hussain Dharani, who had started working there over a month ago. Despite his hectic work schedule, Maqsood found time for his neighbours. He knew them, and they liked him. They remember him embracing Islam all over again in 2000. He offered namaaz regularly and followed the Koran strictly. 'We don't exactly know what happened, but this was a completely new side of him,' recalls Farooq Ansari, treasurer of Sagar Towers, where the Darveshs' reside. Now, wife Shabnam teaches the Koran to young girls every week.

Ramesh Raut

A senior clerk in the education department

Ramesh Raut (53) liked being the man of routine he was. Before leaving for work at 8.30 am, he would sit for his puja for over five hours when he would chant mantras and read out from the Puranas. And every Tuesday, he would make it a point to carry a fresh garland of flowers for the framed portrait of Lord Ganesh that adorned the walls of his office. That day he said he was hurrying as he would not be in the office the next day for some personal reasons. Ramesh, who was from Umrale village on the outskirts of Nallasopara, was a down-to-earth person. His elder brother Suryakant says he never had any addictions or vices. His longtime neighbour and childhood schoolmate Nandkumar Jawle remembers him as a quiet boy. 'During our school days at Vasai, most of the boys would be very naughty during our train commute. However, Ramesh would be quiet and stay seated in one place,' he recalls. He was religious too. 'He would fast on Shankastis and Chaturthis,' his wife Kamini remembers. 'One of his last wishes was to take the family to Goa. Also, he had this desire to travel in a plane at least once in his life!' Kamini misses him and the Sundays they spent together. On Sundays, Ramesh would go to the market and return home with the week's supplies and lots of newspapers which he would devour for the next few hours. 'He was a very homely person and preferred to be in the company of his family,' she says.

Narendra Rawal

An accounts manager, wanted daughters settled

For the Rawals, February 6 was the happiest day of their lives; their elder daughter, Hiral, had married on that day and Narendra (53) felt relieved that one half of his responsibility was finally taken care of. The other half, they prayed, would happen in time. But five months later, Narendra Rawal died in the serial train blasts, leaving his wife Pratiksha to complete what he had vowed to do – see that Palak, their younger daughter, completed her studies successfully and was able to settle down to a happy married life. 'We were partially relieved after Hiral's marriage,' recalls Pratiksha. 'Narendra was happy that Hiral had got a qualified husband and a good family as in-laws.' She says her husband would always encourage Hiral and Palak to study hard as he never wanted them to be dependents. 'He wanted both of them to be educationally qualified and then marry into good families,' she adds. 'It was his biggest concern.' Narendra's mother Daiben can't believe she is alive when her son is no more. She has been bedridden ever since. 'I cannot get over the grief of losing my son,' is all that she manages to say. But both mother and wife try and find comfort in talking about the most important person in their lives. 'He was very meticulous since childhood. He was always good in studies,' his mother remembers. For Pratiksha, who calls him a 'cooperative husband through the 30 years of marriage' Narendra's life was fairly simple. 'He never had to struggle for a job. After completing his graduation in science he got a job in a private company where he worked as accounts manager,' she recalls.

RICHARD D'MONTE

Project manager, was to move to his flat in December

On July 11, Richard D'Monte (37) was returning home with a name for his one-month-old daughter – his final choice after scouring the Internet every day. 'He would download several names, bring them to me and explain the meanings,' says Richard's wife Hedviges. 'Audri was one of the names shortlisted. I never got to know his final choice, so we named her Audri.' For the D'Monte family, Richard's death was the second tragedy in less than a year. Richard's father Augustine had died of a heart attack in November 2005. 'By the time we could cope with that, we had to face this,' says Ruby D'Britto, Richard's younger sister. Richard lived in Ghas village, a few kilometres from Nallasopara station and worked as a project manager for Tyco Fire and Securities, located in Deonar. He specialized in supervising the maintenance of traffic signals. He and Hedviges were planning to move into their new home – a flat closer to Nallasopara station – in December. Hedviges says they had put in a lot of effort to do up their new flat. 'I remember the day we had gone shopping for ceramic tiles for the kitchen,' she says. 'Now, it will not be easy for me to shift there.' Richard and Hedviges were from the same village and had known each other since childhood. They were married eight years ago. 'People say love fades faster in a love marriage, but in our case it grew stronger,' she says. 'He was always helping around at home. If I was busy in the kitchen, he would get our son Gravhil ready for school despite being in a hurry to leave for office.'

HEMANT VAIDYA

A railway booking clerk, he loved to go trekking

Hemant Vaidya (38), head booking clerk at Mumbai Central Railway Station, even missed the quick bhelpuri stop with office colleagues after work that evening. 'He said he was already late and refused to join in,' says Kanwar Bharadwaj, chief booking clerk at Mumbai Central. And he was in such a hurry that he forgot to carry his lunch-box as he rushed off to Nallasopara, where he lived. He returned for the lunch-box, and ended up on board another train targeted by the terrorists. Having joined Western Railway as a junior clerk in 1981, Vaidya was a hard-working employee, say colleagues. Chief Booking Supervisor J.P. Menon, Vaidya's immediate boss at Mumbai Central, recalls that Vaidya would take up every task assigned without complaint. 'Whatever job I gave, he was always ready to do. We lost a good employee,' says Menon. 'His friends say that if he'd stayed back even a few minutes to eat bhelpuri with them, he would have been alive.' Jose Vargees, also posted at Mumbai Central, had boarded the train along with Vaidya, but feeling uneasy in the packed compartment, Vargees alighted at Dadar, one station before the blast. 'Jose was so shocked that he did not come to office until several days later,' says Bharadwaj. They say Vaidya was fond of music, especially old Bollywood numbers. He also loved the hills and often went trekking on trips sponsored by Western Railway. His wife, a senior technician posted in the Doordarshan Kendra in Mumbai, remembers his good nature and willingness to help her, 'But we don't discuss him too much, since our daughter gets upset,' she says. Daughter Uttara is studying in standard IX.

187 MUMBAI LIFE STORIES

Yeshwant Bedekar

A banker who loved history, Marathi theatre

As he lay on the funeral pyre his face looked like it always did, Leena Joshi remembers. Her neighbour's body was covered and she couldn't see his wounds, a severed stump of an arm, a shattered heel. As he lay there, the tall, well-built and impeccably dressed Yeshwant Bedekar's face 'was looking fresh'. There are others who rued the loss of a young life – he was only 45 – and also the passing of an uncommonly wholesome personality, courteous, knowledgeable, beset by angst, wistful. Yeshwant held a mid-level managerial post at the State Bank of India's Worli branch. But his interests did not tend towards banking. He was fond of Marathi theatre and fiction. Home was at Malad, the SBI quarters. On Sunday mornings, he would put on his hunter boots and go for four-hour walks in the Borivali National Park. He liked watching nature and history channels with his young daughter, Aditi. He carried the weight of many expectations. Certainly he'd been a successful student – 27th in the SSC merit list of 1976 and 29th in the armed forces medical examination. The military had refused him because of his poor eyesight. He also tried getting into the Indian Forest Service; it would have taken him into the forests he loved. But by then he was working with SBI and could not take the IFS exam. Years later, Yeshwant often spoke regretfully about his decision, which offered him a monotonous life and no chance to pursue his interests. 'He would often tell me, "My life was over when I took this job." He was not an ordinary man, but he was stuck in an ordinary job,' says his friend Patwardhan.

Ashok Kumar Ajmera

NTC engineer, always cheerful and diligent at work

Ashok Kumar Ajmera (54) could never say no to anyone. '"Yes boss, *ho jayega*" he would say cheerfully whenever I gave him any task,' recalls V.D. Zope, of the National Textile Corporation. So, two years ago too, when he was told to move to the head office to work on a different project, Ajmera, despite being reluctant, couldn't say no. He was then a chief engineer at the Tata Mills in Elphinstone, and had served the better part of his 21-year career with the NTC ensuring the smooth functioning of machines. 'He was quite comfortable with the grease and dirt on his hands. He told me that he was not cut out for a desk job,' says Zope, who convinced Ajmera that the new job would be more challenging than the one he held. Ajmera's brief was to assist senior colleague A.G. Bapat, a consultant with NTC after retirement, in all issues relating to mill land redevelopment. 'He gelled with Bapat very well, and both were a remarkable team, putting in long hours every day,' says Zope. He had taken to the new job as if he had always been made for it, adds N.N. Kamath, Deputy Manager (Management Services) at NTC. 'It was always the challenge in the work that motivated him.' Colleagues recall that everything seemed to be going well for Ajmera. He and his wife Savitri had moved into their new flat, both his sons had good jobs. And he had just become a grandfather. 'Ajmera had a cheerfulness about him that was so contagious that everybody around him felt good,' says P.M. Bidri, a colleague.

Ramankutty Nair

Retired legal firm executive, migrated to Mumbai to build a life

These days, walking with a crutch for support, Chandramathy, who is partially blind after steroids damaged her left eye, finds it difficult to live without the man who stood by her through 'good times and bad'. Ramankutty (65) died in the July 11 blast at Mahim station on his way back home from his part-time job at the legal firm LC Tolat & Company – a position he had taken after retiring from there as an executive-cum-stenographer in 2001. His family found his body a day later in the morgue at Sion hospital. 'I always feared for his life. Our family astrologer, who had predicted that I would lose my left eye, had also said he would die when he turned 65. I had kept it to myself, praying every day that it should not come true,' says Chandramathy. During their early years in Mumbai, Ramankutty and Chandramathy lived with his elder brother in Navy Nagar in Colaba. He shifted to Malad, a Mumbai suburb, a year later and settled down in Kurar village in the area. As she talks about her various illnesses over the years – tuberculosis, diabetes and kidney complications – that 'drained the family's finances' Chandramathy also narrates how Ramankutty would be by her side to comfort her, never once showing 'disrespect or discomfort because of her chronic illnesses'. While ensuring that she was taken to every hospital, from JJ to Jaslok to Hinduja, he also enjoyed cooking for her – 'soft chappatis and finely-chopped vegetables, with just the right amount of salt…he would always yell from the kitchen to ask me, "Chandu, what else do you want?"'

Hemchandra Mastakar

Retired finance officer, was Mr Fix-it at home

The elders had arranged their marriage. That was the beginning of their love affair. For, Suvarna and Hemchandra Mastakar (65) complemented each other in the best of ways: he was diplomatic, she was forthright; he was Mr Fix-it of the house while her forte was in academics. Married to him, Suvarna thought God had finally answered her prayers. Her husband was all that she had wanted him to be, and more. He was considerate, practical, fun to be with and, above all, a good father to their children. And all he ever wanted from her were spotless (without the burn marks) chappatis. That was how uncomplicated their life together was and Suvarna had thought it was for keeps. Today, Hemchandra Mastakar, isn't alive. He died in the 7/11 train blasts. After 35 years of spending their lives together, Suvarana shares a secret. Those chappatis, she says, were not always spotless. And when those black burn marks did appear in some – no matter how hard she tried to prevent them – she would discreetly pinch them out. Says Suvarna, 'In one moment my *jodidhar* was taken away, just like that. How do you expect me to cope? My life is shattered and I have lost my faith in God.' But Suvarna tries to change her mood by talking about her husband and his 'exceptional skills' with all things mechanical. 'He could repair a watch, any electric or electronic gadget and even do a good job of designing the interiors of our home. His father was a watchmaker, but he didn't pick up anything from him as he died when Hemchandra was only seven. It must have been in his genes,' she says.

187 MUMBAI LIFE STORIES

HIMMATLAL PRABHUDAS MODI

His employer wouldn't let him retire

Himmatlal's valuations of cotton never went wrong. So, his employer Damodar Seth did not allow him to retire – he wanted him to continue coming to office, even if only for four hours, according to his convenience. Himmatlal Prabhudas Modi (65) willingly agreed. That day on 7/11, he boarded a train as usual from Churchgate for Malad. 'His earlier office was at Cotton Green. But now they had shifted near Cotton Exchange,' recalls wife Shantaben who is still struggling to come to terms with what has happened. 'Himmatbhai came to Mumbai from Saurashtra in the sixties. His family was in the business of cotton trading and hence as a quality control expert, his valuations were always accurate.' It's been a difficult time for the family of four daughters, their husbands, and their lone son, Mehul. A diehard cricket fan, Himmatlal would always be glued to the television whenever there was a cricket match on. At the Kuwawala chawl, he was popular for his kindness and was known for never refusing anyone who asked him for help. 'He was a thorough gentleman and I am not saying this just because he was my papa,' says Sangita as she looks at the TV set that's been switched off and is kept covered ever since he died. The railways offered a class four job to the family who thought Mehul would be the best suited for it. Unfortunately, he did not fulfil the minimum qualification criteria and couldn't take it up. But now Mehul has managed to find work elsewhere with a transport company in Khetwadi.

Nandkumar Vaidya

BMC senior inspector, known for diplomacy

Famous for his receding hairline and hair dyed jet black, Nandkumar Vaidya (56) was equally well known for his diplomacy. To function well as a senior inspector in the BMC's licences department you need to know the knack of appeasing people – confronting angry bosses, calming irate applicants unhappy about the paperwork, or gently coercing corporators. When you entered his cabin (a little enclosure with wooden partitions and posters of impossibly picturesque woodland scenes on the wall) Vaidya would take away the sting from anything he had to say to you by first offering a cup of tea: 'First, relax. Then tell me what you are so worked up about. What, that's all? Hand in these papers. Let me see what I can do.' More often than not, the visitor would exit calmer than he was, recall colleagues Eknath Dhayalkar and Sanjay Patil. In the few months he worked at the Parel office, colleagues began to like him for his friendly nature and respect him for his methodical approach to work. Despite his seniority, Nandkumar thought nothing of putting an arm around the shoulders of junior colleagues and sharing their snacks with them. In office Nandkumar would note down in his diary the names and telephone numbers of each and every visitor. Also, he would obsess about finishing all his assignments and often stay back until the last staffer had left. 'Nandkumar's forte lay in inter-personal relations: he knew how to deal with bosses. He knew the smallest detail about the department and would answer each query coming from above,' says Patil, an inspector of advertising licences, who often looked to Vaidya for advice.

MANOJ SHAH

Diamond trader, wife and son have left for Nashik

All of seven, Yash has stopped playing his favourite game, cricket. For his best buddy, with whom he shared this passion, is no more. His father, Manoj Shah (38), a diamond trader, died in the 7/11 blasts. A well-established diamond trader, Manoj ran his family business from the Shukra Complex in Malad and Panchratna at Opera House, the hub of the diamond business in Mumbai. That day, Manoj was carrying diamonds worth Rs 5 lakh with him in a pouch when he died in the blasts at Jogeshwari. Constables S.T. Khanvilkar and Mahesh Kadam who were on duty at 11 pm that night, found the diamonds. A week later, they traced the diamonds to Manoj and returned them to his wife. Neighbours at the Mahudi Mansion, Malad, where the Shahs used to live, remember them as a picture-perfect family. '*Hamara Manoj bhai ne kabhi kisi ka kuch nahi bigada*,' says watchman Nensingh Thapa. Friends miss Manoj. 'I lost a good neighbour,' says Pravin Prajapati. 'These days, whenever we receive a call enquiring about ticket bookings for Saurashtra, I am reminded of him. For Manoj bhai would ask about the same booking from his balcony, which is just above our office.' After Manoj's death, it was getting increasingly difficult for wife Archana to live in the same house. She has since moved to Nashik where Yash has started going to school. Once a fortnight, she comes to Mumbai to visit her sister's family in Malad. A busy professional by day and family man by night, that is how Archana will always remember her husband. And no, Yash doesn't play much cricket any more.

Nilesh Paurana

An engineer, wanted to create software of his own

Nilesh Paurana (42) a software engineer, spoke to his wife Gauri at 5.45 pm on 7/11, minutes before the first class compartment of the 5.17 Virar Fast he was travelling in exploded. He was returning home from work at Nariman Point. 'He had reached Bandra by then,' Gauri says. So, she was unaware about the blasts until her sister told her about them. Gauri says Nilesh was a 'keep safe kind of person', one who never took risks in life. Just the other day, he had decided to take the day off fearing riots in Mumbai after the desecration of a statue of Meenatai Thackeray. A caring husband, he was also a thorough professional at work, and always ready to help others. 'He dreamt of one day creating his own software, but that will remain a dream now,' says Gauri, a doctor by profession. After going to the Bhayander blast site that evening she went to a hospital, where her husband had succumbed to his injuries. Their eight-year-old daughter Ruchi has still not recovered from the shock. 'Ruchi misses his presence. Every now and then she says that if her dad was here they would have done this or that together,' says Gauri. But the tragedy has lent her a maturity beyond her years. Ruchi cares for her mother and grandmother like a grown-up. Now Gauri is determined to fulfil Nilesh's other dream – to see their daughter become a surgeon. His mother, who is 73, has lost two sons earlier – one in an accident and the other to a heart attack. Nilesh was her third and last son. 'She has suffered a lot in her life. Nilesh's death is too much for her to bear,' says Gauri.

FRANCIS LOBO

His daughter was his jaan

On July 11, Judy had tried persuading her husband Francis Lobo (48) to skip work; he had viral fever and a bad cold. But Francis told her he had to attend an important meeting in his office, Datamatrix, an overseas recruiting firm in Colaba, where he had been working for the last 28 years. He never returned. 'Everyone in the building returned home safe, except my husband.' On his way home to IC Colony, Borivali, Francis was caught in the blast on a train near Khar station. A homemaker, Judy says she was 'completely dependent' on Francis, particularly because she often fell ill, being an insulin-dependent diabetic. And he would always be there to take care of her. 'I used to tell him, "I will die before you." I have always been in bed, needing medication for the past 14 years. Now I have to take good care of myself for my daughter's sake. I am only worried about her future,' says Judy. Recently, when Judy was cleaning a cupboard, she found Francis's promotion letter. It moved her. 'He was a very efficient employee and had brought much business to the company. He received so many best employee awards,' she says proudly. 'There was something very special about him. In a job where stress levels are high, he was the most relaxed person,' says Subhash Bhatia, the CEO of Datamatrix. These days, Judy Lobo is struggling to celebrate Christmas for her young daughter's sake; her happiness was so important to Francis. But every time she sees the brightly lit shops and the happy families milling around, she thinks of the happiness that is over for her.

ARUN PATOLE

Worked by day and studied at night to become an engineer

Arun Patole (36) was like any other struggling Mumbaiite, a man who had worked hard throughout his life so that he could move out of his BDD chawl in Worli to a two-bedroom home in Nallasopara. Yet, talking about him to his family and friends, one discovers an altogether different Arun; a young uncle who loved to be the mischievous Mamaji to his nephews; a man who secretly donated funds for his village. Arun got himself a diploma in engineering and then enrolled in night classes at Sardar Vallabbhai Patel College to earn an engineering degree. All the while, he had a day job to keep. 'He was under a lot of pressure to work – he had three sisters to look after,' says brother-in-law Nandkumar Bane, a telephone operator with the railways. But his hard work eventually paid off. And, finally, Arun became a civil engineer and joined the BMC. 'He was such a workaholic that many a time we had to actually go out to look for him and bring him home. Often, we shouted at him for his carelessness, for not informing us about his whereabouts,' says Bane who insists on being called his brother. Bane recalls his favourite line: 'Since I am the youngest of all, pay my bus ticket.' But, while eating out in hotels, none of them would have the slightest idea that he had already paid at the counter before they had even started eating. Working in BMC meant Arun had to deal with various kinds of people. But he never lost his temper. 'He remained in touch with his chawl friends and often went there to celebrate Gokulashtami, Holi and other festivals.'

Sandeep Zavar

A company secretary who never stopped learning

An avid academic, Sandeep Zawar (33) was the diligent kind: even while managing work, he found the strength and enthusiasm to pursue a career enhancement course. But his life wasn't about all work and no play. He loved driving his car. Sadly, Sandeep's dreams came crashing on 7/11 when he died in the train blast at Khar. Wife Pooja hasn't yet come to terms with his death. So, she and their three-year-old son have left Mumbai. 'What can I say? It's too hard for me to even think about it. You can imagine what Pooja is going through,' says Kalpana, the wife of Sandeep's elder brother, Sudhir. The Zawar family came to Mumbai from their village in Rajasthan to make a better living for themselves more than a decade ago. They were doing well. Sandeep worked as a freelance company secretary operating from his office in Malad and Sudhir was employed with Siyaram Textiles. Till two years ago, they'd lived together as one happy family – Sandeep, Pooja, their son, and Sudhir, Kalpana and their two children – in a flat in Jesal Park in Bhayander. 'Sandeep was a very responsible and punctual person,' recalls Kalpana. 'Even if it was a matter of getting late by ten minutes, he would call and inform us.' Maybe that's why the family began worrying early that day – but they did not hear anything about Sandeep till late at night. 'I saw him at least twice a day while he was going and returning from work,' says his friend Ramesh Akhani, who owns a medicine shop, and likes to describe his friend of ten years as a well-educated, intelligent person with a knack for solving problems.

Krishna Kumar Parasnath

A banker and a badminton player

Krishna Parasnath's apartment in Malad has been locked up. His wife, Anju, who was expecting their second child, couldn't bear to stay there any more. Today, five months after 7/11 shattered her family, she has been blessed with a son, their second. And they all live in Powai with her brother. 'You know, Krishna was so excited about the prospect of a new family member in his house,' says his friend and colleague at Indian Overseas Bank, Rakesh Kumar. Anju delivered a baby boy in September. But she left the house as it brought back too many memories. The 'star' of their housing society – Indian Overseas Bank Apartments in Malad – Krishna (37) was at the forefront of each and every social event or festival, and now he is being sorely missed. Most so by Kumar as they were both from Bihar. And both the 'Bihar ka babus' loved to laugh about the fact that they were in Mumbai to earn a better living. 'He came from Motipur, a small town in Bihar, in 2001. And I landed here in 2003. But ever since I got to know him, I stopped missing Bihar. We chatted in our typically Bihari accents and spoke of a number of things like our hometowns and the special delicacies we missed here,' reminisces Kumar. But it wasn't their roots alone that brought them close. Badminton played a part too. 'Krishna was an amazing badminton player,' recalls Kumar. 'We had been partners since 2003. Every year, our Society conducts a badminton championship and we took part. Though we never won doubles, we did get a cup in the singles,' he laughs.

Lalit Kachalia

A jeweller, son wants to be a pilot

Lalit Kachalia (41) did not die in the bomb blasts of July 11. His wife and two children will never let him die. He continues to be a vital part of the simple, uncomplicated life of the family he left behind. At their residence at Kandivali Mahaveer Nagar, there are no tell-tale signs of a grieving household to explain the absence of the lone earning member of the family. Vandana does not use the 'D' word about her late husband. Everything in the household seems uncannily normal. Unless one has prior knowledge about how Lalit, a jeweller, was found among the dead after the 7/11 train blasts and was duly cremated by the family, there is no way of knowing. 'We firmly believe he is out there somewhere and will return to us someday,' says Vandana. Mother of two – Shoubit (16) and Krupa (9) – she hasn't yet 'touched' the Rs 5 lakh railway ex gratia and the Rs 1 lakh state government compensation. It's not that she doesn't need money but accepting such 'help' is something her late husband would not have approved of. Initially, she was even reluctant to accept the money. It was only after family members persuaded her that she agreed. 'My husband had a strong sense of pride and always wanted to lead a dignified life and not find himself in a situation where he would have to accept favours from others. My children are young and impressionable. If I take others help now, they will never learn to stand on their feet,' she says with conviction. Son Shoubit wants to be a pilot. His determination to become one is fuelled by the fact that his father always hoped that he would.

Manish Manihar

An MBA graduate who wanted to join the IAS

Only a month before he died, Manish Manihar (26) had shifted from his job with the American Express Bank, to BLB Limited – the salary package was more lucrative. Till today, his family regrets that move. Had he been with his earlier employers, he might not have been on one of the ill-fated trains of 7/11, they believe. The Vasai resident, an MBA from Pune University, was on his way home on board the 6.17 pm Virar Local from Churchgate in the compartment that exploded at Mahim. 'He never left his office before 7 pm,' says Ramesh Manihar his father. 'That day, somehow, he left early.' As the only male offspring in the extended family – Ramesh's two sisters and three brothers all have daughters – Manish was somewhat special. But he was determined not to let his sister's education lag behind his. 'He studied very hard,' says Ramesh, 'and he was very keen that his sister and his cousins too become something in life.' His sister, now married, is a chartered accountant. 'All due to his efforts.' Manish, who loved snacking on vada-pav and took a special interest in astrology, had been married only for four months. Ramesh recounts an incident that, for him, describes his son most aptly: 'There is a woman who sells utensils in our locality. When she heard the news of Manish's passing away, she began weeping, and telling us how well-mannered Manish had always been. One day, quite unexpectedly, he had touched her feet asking for her blessings. That's what Manish was like.'

Kumud Shah

A diamond broker, he loved to travel

As a Hindi news channel broadcast live pictures from the Jogeshwari blast, one close-up caught their eye. A driving licence with Kumud Shah's name on it. At 18, son Neeraj Shah had a brutal introduction to adulthood. He and his family went from one hospital to another, sifting through the dead, until they finally reached Cooper hospital's morgue where an unclaimed body waited for them. The face was damaged, but Neeraj identified his father from the gold chain around his neck, his clothes and his shoes. For Kumud Shah(48), a diamond merchant by profession, the ride from their Borivali apartment to Charni Road, to the diamond bourse at Panchratna, Opera House, was part of his daily routine. He had been fasting that day as it was Guru Purnima and had phoned wife Unnati at 5:30 pm to inform her he was on his way home. 'I can't get the right words to describe Dad,' Neeraj says emotionally, then begins to describe a loving father who doted on him and his sister Ankita. 'He was not at all strict with us, he was very lenient, very caring,' Neeraj says. Kumud would often frequent the religious shrines of the 24 tirthankaras of the Jain faith. A travel freak, he would also ensure the family got a fun-filled summer vacation each year. Though the joint family is cushioning the blow for Shah's young son and daughter it is not easy for them. Friends and acquaintances will always remember him for the cultured upbringing he gave Neeraj and Ankita. Polite and courteous even in their grief, the children he was so proud of, want only to grow up to be like him.

187
MUMBAI
LIFE STORIES

Shashi Shekhar Singh

Central excise inspector, just needed an excuse to celebrate

At the Dadar headquarters of the Central Excise Commissionerate (Division Thane II), they mourn the loss of two colleagues, working in different departments, but sitting an arm's length from each other. Shashi Shekhar Singh (37) was the good-natured, cheerful, raring-to-go, excise inspector in the adjudication section whose open-hearted smile they all sorely miss. Asha Shashikant, the inspector now handling Shashi's work and occupying his chair, can't forget the morning of that ill-fated day. 'My son's standard X results were out,' she says. And as soon as she walked in, Shashi wanted to celebrate. 'No mithai? Don't step in,' he had joked. Nelson Fernando, superintendent and one of Shashi's immediate seniors, adds: 'He just needed an excuse to celebrate, to order sweets. He loved sweets.' P.V. Ramchandran, another superintendent in the same office had been on the same train but luckily he was in another compartment. 'Shashi always rose to the occasion when targets had to be met,' he remembers. With no fresh recruitment and responsibilities multiplying, it's common for central excise inspectors to work late. 'Just the previous day, he'd stayed back till 8 pm; we were getting some show-cause notices prepared and signed by the boss from his residence,' says Fernando. 'That's why we asked him to leave on time the next day.' Shashi's wife is now working as a tax assistant, an out-of-turn appointment made on compassionate grounds by the Central Excise Commissionerate for her and the wife of Sanjay Samant, their other officer who was killed in the blasts.

Subhash Sawant

Bank employee and Sena member, loved helping people

Subhash Sawant (45) worshipped Bal Thackeray. A member of the Shiv Sena for over 14 years, he was content being a party worker, never wanting to run for office, not even for a corporator's position. For some time, though, he was a vice-president in the local municipal ward unit in Nallasopara, a Mumbai suburb. What he enjoyed doing most was to help people, and he was always willing to help them sort out their routine problems: like in the payment of bills and battling an intermittent water supply, says Shirish Chavan, president of the Sena's local taluka unit. And Sawant found time for all of this while working for a cooperative bank in the Fort area. His sons Kunal and Pranay are proud that their father was an office-bearer in the Shiv Sena. But Kunal says he has not yet decided whether he will follow in his footsteps. Like many Nallasopara residents, Sawant commuted to his bank in Fort daily by train. He lived in a small flat. In his living room, Thackeray's portrait is prominently displayed. Despite his admiration for Thackeray, Sawant had, of late, distanced himself from the Sena. Apparently, some of his neighbours had said his building was not getting enough water because of his political affiliations. Sawant also resigned from his party post. But he continued to support his party from the outside, said colleagues who did not want to be quoted. 'He had not broken ties (with the party),' one of them said, 'even though he sometimes had to support other parties as well on local issues.'

Lalit Raghu Kakani

A shy and reticent diamond merchant, who loved cricket

The New Year spirit got to Rachna. While Mumbai would join the rest of the world welcoming the new year, she realized it would be difficult for her to remain in the Andheri apartment she once shared with her husband – she would miss her husband, Lalit Kakani (27) more than ever before. So, she and her seven-month-old son packed their bags to spend the last few days of December '06 in Jodhpur with her mother. At least Jodhpur is far removed from Mumbai, once the city of their dreams, and now the city in which she lost her husband to the 7/11 train blasts. Their neighbour, Meera Goradia, says that Rachna went into a shell after what happened. Now they all miss the 'quiet Kakanis': from security guard Uttam Chandra to those working at Harish Chandra Chana Bhandar, the nearest grocery shop. 'The seven years I have been working here, I was always greeted with a smile from Lalit – as if he was telling me everything is finel,' recalls Chandra, the guard of Shivam Apartments, adding, 'Kakani saab was reserved. Only on Sundays, he would be out on the lawns of our complex. And I would get a handshake.' Lalit, a diamond merchant, was returning home from his Opera House office on July 11 when he died in the blast at Jogeshwari station. Today, neighbours and friends remember him fondly. They reminisce about his shy nature, his lovely smile, his naughty wink and his love for cricket. 'Not many people are calm and reserved yet loving,' says Meera Goradia. 'Though, he never said it, we knew we could count on him if we needed help.'

187
MUMBAI
LIFE STORIES

Dushyant Madhukar Bhoir

A talented musician, got a full-time job a month ago

Only a month ago, Dushyant Madhukar Bhoir (29), a resident of Bhayander, had shifted from his earlier temporary job in Air India to a permanent job in a firm at Dadar. 'We thought he was well-settled. But now we have lost him,' says Madhukar Bhoir, Dushyant's father. Describing Dushyant as gregarious and energetic, the proud father boasts about his son's keen interest – and talent – in music. 'He used to play a lot of musical instruments. The guitar was his favourite. He managed to perform with some orchestras and earn some decent money on the side.' Usually he left office after 7 pm but that day he and his wife had some plans. So he left office early to board a train. He was killed in the blast at Matunga. 'One of his friends, who missed that train, told us what happened,' recalls Bhoir. 'We found his body at Sion hospital.' Apart from his wife, father and mother, Dushyant leaves behind a younger brother and an elder sister. Yet, for Bhoir, the vacuum is too deep to fill. 'Some days back I went to a musical programme and when I saw the percussionists performing on stage, I was reminded of my son. Not only do I miss him when I see someone performing, but I actually miss him every second.' Dushyant's grandmother Rukmini who stays in her village home at Mori in Naigaon, describes him as a well-mannered and hard-working youngster. 'He was always smiling. Why did it happen to him?' she asks. Bhoir, a mechanic with Central Railway, was dealt a double blow when Dushyant's wife, Varsha, decided to return to her parents' home.

Jaykumar Nair

Loved to dance and have fun

At a Christian wedding march accompanied by music, guests are expected to join the newly-weds and walk in pairs. So when the music started to play at a July '05 wedding on Mira Road, it was but natural for Jaykumar Nair (55) to ask his 'neighbourhood girlfriend' to join him as partner. Between waltz, foxtrot and jive, Jaykumar and Waveney Periera had 'the time of their life, dancing and competing with the young crowd'. This last dance serves as Pereira's abiding memory of her dear friend. 'I will always cherish the fun, frolic and laughter of that evening,' says the widow, a social science teacher at Our Lady of Good Counsel, Sion. Jaykumar, a former director of a private firm, died in the 7/11 train blasts on his way back home from Churchgate. Neighbours at his Mira Road Sector 10 apartment know little about him. 'He was a loner, estranged from his wife and family,' is all they can offer. For Pereira, Jaykumar's death means she has lost a good friend, the 'jovial Mallu' who would peep in and check on her, at times even walk to her door to hand over the society's maintenance charges and bring her banana wafers whenever he came back from a trip to Kerala. Of late, Jaykumar had decided to invest in a rubber plantation, reveals a close friend. In June 2006, he'd also made up his mind to cut down on his frequent trips to Kerala. Mumbai would be his home, and he was getting ready to explore it more closely in his old Maruti 800. In fact, he'd even shaved off his trademark moustache. 'Don't I look ten years younger?' he'd asked his friends, smiling jauntily.

187 MUMBAI LIFE STORIES

Jogarao Mantri Pagada

Bank employee, neighbours barely knew him

They barely knew him, exchanged no pleasantries apart from an occasional polite nod and didn't miss him when he failed to show up for gatherings organized in the suburban apartment complex where he lived for six months. So, when Jogarao Mantri Pagada (50) died in one of the serial bomb blasts on board the suburban local trains on July 11, 2006, residents of Goregaon's Riddhi Garden felt only a quiet loss, perhaps some wished they'd known him better. A tall, strapping man, fair-complexioned, he had a striking presence, they say. A bank employee, he had shifted to his new residence, a rented accommodation provided by his employer, only six months prior to the tragedy. With no family nearby and almost no friends in Mumbai, his family – wife and young son – has since returned to his hometown in Andhra Pradesh. Jogarao was an early riser, says Shankar Mistry Naidu, the security guard at Riddhi Gardens. 'Before 8.30 am, he'd be out, heading to work. And in the six months that he was here, he never once broke that routine.' Perhaps he was a workaholic, neighbours muse, since he also almost never returned home before 9.30 pm. Building residents say Jogarao's family packed their belongings from their fifth floor rented apartment and left for Hyderabad in September, after completing formalities with Western Railway. They left no forwarding address – Mumbai had not been kind to them.

Girish Talpade

Celebrated granddaughter's birthday two days before death

In a television commercial, a grandfather gifts his grandson a bicycle for his birthday. Nothing unusual for most viewers, but for ten-year-old Aditi Talpade, that ad spells heartbreak. Manager at the Mega Safe Deposit Lockers Company, Girish Talpade (68) had given his little granddaughter Aditi a bicycle for her birthday on July 9. It was just the gift Aditi had wanted and she was the happiest girl alive.Two days later, her darling grandfather was gone. He died in the train blast at Matunga station. Aditi cannot come to terms with her loss. This year, Talpade had gone out of his way to make Aditi's birthday special. He had a half-day on Saturday, so he went shopping for return gifts at Crawford Market. 'He was really enthusiastic. He bought dozens of fancy items, even though we were not going to have a huge party. Then he decorated the hall with confetti and gifts. Two days later he was gone. It is unbelievable,' says his daughter-in-law, Anjali. The ever-active Talpade was born and brought up in suburban Vile Parle. He completed his education in Mumbai and graduated as an engineer. Reminiscing about all the years they shared together, his school friend Arvind Kasargod says, 'Girish and I had been together since our kindergarten days at the Chitale Bainchee Shaalaa in Vile Parle. We then studied together in Parle Tilak Vidyalay till SSC. I remember him most for his straight-faced one-liners.'

LOUIS SEQUERIA

A diehard fan of vegetarian food

Twenty-eight years ago, when Louis Sequeria (58) first saw Clara's photograph in his cousin's wedding album, he was charmed by her simple yet elegant looks. So smitten was he that he immediately tried getting in touch with her, asking friends and common acquaintances to introduce them formally. But when that didn't work out, he barged into her office – actor Sunil Dutt's establishment in Bandra – and introduced himself. 'We first danced together on January 1 at someone else's wedding in 1979 and tied the knot in October the same year,' says Clara, with a smile. 'A diehard fan of vegetarian food', Louis made it a point that Clara cooked his food exactly the way it tasted in his Gujarati colleague's tiffin. 'I would get irritated with him sometimes when he demanded vegetarian food even in the evenings,' says Clara. 'We need fish curry and rice at least once a day, I would tell him.' But Louis knew how to calm his wife and make her laugh: 'He always sang *Jab koi baat bigad jaye* and down went my temper.' Three years ago, Louis met with a serious accident when his car rammed into a van, 'but he first rescued the driver and then got himself admitted to hospital,' remembers Clara. While son Ashley works in Qatar, daughter Sarena, studying in St Andrew's College, is her mother's strongest support. She says, 'Daddy loved old songs. Most days, after prayers and playing solitaire on the computer, he would slip into his own world where there was just him and his small transistor.' Now, his wife and daughter say, the music has gone out of their lives.

SUDHIR CHIMOTE

Loved ghazals, and his granddaughter

For Sudhir Chimote (59), there was only one way to live life – to live it large and to be happy. This attitude of his was contagious wherever he went and everyone around him was affected by it. He was almost like Santa Claus in his gregariousness but without the red suit and potbelly. 'My father was young at heart. He loved to live life,' recalls son Shukrit. 'He was very optimistic, outgoing and carefree. Quite unlike us,' admits his son, now based in Princeton, New Jersey. So, when he came here in July to perform his father's last rites, he wasn't surprised in the least when his father's colleagues told him how the office atmosphere would lighten up the moment Sudhir would arrive. Sudhir loved music, especially ghazals, and absolutely doted on his granddaughter. He completed his graduation in his hometown of Nagpur, and fell in love with a Bengali girl, Krishna, in his neighbourhood. They were married in 1972. Weekends were typical. Sudhir would step out for a walk in the morning and chat up any familiar face he met on the way. 'Our relationship was of friends. I would confide in him things that boys would confide in their friends. In fact, my first drink was with my father,' says Shukrit. The family says that the last seven months before 7/11 had brought about a change in Sudhir. He had started taking an interest in religious matters and would often join wife Krishna when she went to attend the ISKCON discourses. In fact, just a week before the tragedy, the couple had visited Vrindavan.

NITESH PATEL

A keen learner, with a penchant for detail

On July 11 Nitesh Kumar Patel (27), an ambitious young man from Hajipur, completed two years of probation with the Oriental Bank of Commerce in Mumbai and was confirmed as an officer. Nitesh was in retail operations. But colleague Diana Mathias says he always wanted to be in the Foreign Exchange department and remembers him as a keen learner with a penchant for detail. 'I miss his smile,' she adds. Nitesh was good with markets and trading. 'He was always telling me to invest,' recalls friend Yoginder Kumar Barnwal. 'But I never took the risks he so often did.' Colleagues like Sriram Peri admired him for cracking the accounting exam in his first attempt even though he was from the science stream. 'Nitesh hated to commute from his Opera House office to Malad,' says his wife of four months, Nitu. 'He didn't like those overcrowded trains and so New Delhi, where he worked for a year before moving to Mumbai, was his first choice.' When Nitesh joined OBC in March 2005, he made friends easily. On that day, his colleagues did what his family would have, fanning out in groups to search for him and identifying his body with the help of his ID card and wallet in Sion hospital in the early morning. 'Six or seven of us had gone for lunch that day and I was teasing him,' recalls friend Barnwal. The two of them had hit it off well: 'Being from the same district in Bihar helped us bond, I think.' Since July 11, Nitesh's office friends haven't gone out in a group for lunch. Nor do they have much of an appetite for their earlier, light-hearted, lunchtime banter.

187 MUMBAI LIFE STORIES

A.T. Vinod

SBI manager, wife got an e-mail from him after he died

In Mahe, an outpost of Puducherry inside Kerala, several days after her husband's funeral, Vedapathy opened her e-mail and was stunned. There was a mail from her husband A.T. Vinod (46), dated July 11, the very day his body was dragged out of the mangled first class compartment of the Bandra Borivali Fast. 'We never sent mails to each other when we were together. I did not know what to expect. There was no reason for him to have sent me an e-mail,' she says. Her husband, a manager with State Bank of India, had sent her a brief message which talked about the future, ending rather prophetically with, 'The Future is Yours.' 'The last time I spoke to A.T. was when he called me at 10.30 am on July 11. He wanted me to cook chicken, Kerala fashion. He loved food.' Their eight-year-old daughter spoke to him at 3.30 pm that day. That evening all his favourite food, remained untouched on the dining table, as Veda paced the floor of their Borivali apartment through the night and her elder brother Rakesh and nephew Rohit frantically searched the hospitals. 'I firmly believed he would be injured, not dead. At 5 am the next day, when I talked to Rakesh he told me he was at the morgue. Now I am trying hard to think of some incident with my husband that will make me angry so that I will not feel so much pain. But, I cannot. He was a lovely person, gentle, patient and simple, like a child. He was unlike a typical Indian male. He gave me space, even though he didn't expect the same from me. I have only wonderful memories of him. And those are so much harder to forget,' says Vedapathy.

Mahipal Parihar

First year B.Com student, wanted to be a CA

Unlike most other boys his age, Mahipal Parihar (19) was very focused on what he wanted to achieve in life. He also took his first step towards his dream of ensuring an easy, well-provided-for life to his family by enrolling for chartered accountancy coaching classes. 'He always wanted to be a CA,' says his father Madanlal Parihar, who works in the railways. A first year B.Com student, he was a regular at both his college and coaching class at Andheri. He would dedicate more than 12 hours to study. At his coaching classes, a huge board mentioning his death also highlights his entrance marks. 'Mahipal was diligent and studious. He attended his classes regularly although he stayed at Nallasopara,' said J.K. Shah, principal of J.K. Shah Classes where Mahipal was preparing for his chartered accountancy. Shah refunded Mahipal's fees to his parents after his death. According to Katchi V.I., principal of Bhavan's College, Andheri, 'As per our records, Mahipal was a student who attended his lectures regularly and was sincere in his studies. He was a simple, quiet boy.' His father says, 'Mahipal, my daughter, my wife and I were a happy family. Being elder to his sister, he was very responsible and mature.' Mahipal had few friends. David Tyagrajan of the neighbourhood is one of them. He remembers him as a responsible boy. 'Even though I was five years older to him, my mother always said he was more mature than me and liked him more.' The two of them shared many confidences; and Tyagrajan can't help smiling as he recalls how they'd tease each other about girls.

187
MUMBAI
LIFE STORIES

Bhogilal Sarvayya

A diamond businessman, had come here 18 yrs ago

Bhogilal Sarvayya (55) was one of the many from Vasai who died in the July 11 serial train blasts last year. His family, originally from Bhavnagar district in Gujarat, came to the island city 18 years ago and has been living here ever since. He is survived by his wife Bhavna, son Pratish and daughter Jalpa. Six months have passed, but Pratish remembers the day vividly. 'I came home early. Late in the evening, my uncle Bipinkaka, who worked in the diamond business at Charni with my father, called to ask if everyone had reached home safe. My father hadn't reached by then.' That's when the family started to panic. 'Much later, I got a call from the police. They asked about my father and asked me who I was. Then, they asked to speak to someone elder in the family. Finally, they broke the news that his body was at Bhagwati hospital.' Ganpat Singh, another neighbour, recalls Bhogilal as a 'quiet man'. Friend M.V. Gawkar calls him a 'polite and humble' person. Bhogilal loved sweets. He did not need festivals as an excuse. 'He would indulge himself without any qualms,' says Pratish. 'He never feared diabetes.' Pratish, who works at Panchratna at Opera House, the hub of the city's diamond business, has taken over the responsibility of the family, while his sister Jalpa, a commerce graduate, is usually at home with her mother. Their soft-spoken mother Bhavna takes one day at a time. Bhogilal loved to travel. He loved to go on pilgrimages with a big group of friends and relatives. This way, says Pratish, he had visited several temples all over India.

187 MUMBAI LIFE STORIES

JITENDRA THADESHWAR

Dealt in artificial jewellery, came to Mumbai three decades ago

To everyone who knew him, Jitendra Thadeshwar (52) or Jitubhai was the unsung ambassador of peace. No, Jitendra Thadeshwar did not appear on TV and he wasn't famous. But in his own way, he embodied peace. To his family, he was no less than a hero. 'He was the *mukhiya* of our house. He was the thread that kept us together under one roof,' says Hiren, his eldest son. 'Though people say time heals all wounds, for us each passing day has been a torment.' Jitubhai belonged to the goldsmith community of Chavand village in Gujarat's Amreli district. He came to Bombay three decades ago and had been living in Kandivali ever since. Jitendra dealt in artificial jewellery, getting work done through skilled craftsmen. Only Hiren has carried on that legacy, while Haresh and Sameer pursue other occupations. Jitubhai, who enjoyed reading and solving crosswords, was a man of commitment. Once he gave his word, he would fulfil his commitment. And, if he was unable to keep his word, he would admit it. 'It was this trait that he tried to inculcate in all his children,' says son Haresh. The family always knew he was a benevolent man. But it was only after his death that they realized he had helped several families monetarily. Jitendra was in a Borivali-bound train in the first class compartment when a bomb exploded in it near Santa Cruz station. He was taken to Cooper hospital. 'We are middle-class people. We have nothing to do with the agenda of terrorists. Why people like my father were targeted is a question for which we are yet to get an answer,' says Haresh.

Yateen Mehta

An engineer, drew strength from spirituality

Yateen Mehta (36) was a civil engineer, but spirituality was the centre of his existence. So much so that it's left a deep impression on his family and colleagues. 'He would always say, "You can't become a spiritual person by genuflecting in front of idols of all the gods. Helping someone and then telling the whole world about it will also not work. The essence of spirituality lies in respecting everything living, non-living or dead. And by helping people without making them realize you are helping them,"' remembers Yateen's wife, Alpa. She says she remembers his words whenever she misses him most. Yateen worked for the Brihanmumbai Municipal Corporation (BMC). 'He always said that by respecting and helping everyone, a person can achieve so much more than those who abandon their families for those cold mountains,' says Alpa. She also points out that Yateen practised what he preached: 'He would often bring home children of labourers from his construction site and we would treat them to a good meal. Also, he loved feeding birds.' His colleagues say Yateen's philosophy showed in his work: he was always associated with the BMC's philanthropic activities. Alpa says now she has just two objectives in life. First, to walk the spiritual path carved out by Yateen. Second, to help their ten-year-old son Kushal to study hard and become a civil engineer, just like his father. 'We have no sense of revenge or bitterness after July 11. We just want to live a simple life like my husband did,' says Alpa, tears rolling down her cheeks.

N. GIRIBABU

A software engineer; wife is still studying

For N. Giribabu (31), a software engineer from a tiny village in Andhra Pradesh, home could really only be down South. But having landed a job in a reputed software firm's Mumbai office, he rented a flat in the vast expanse of realty affordable to migrants to Mumbai, in Vasant Nagri in Nallasopara, over an hour's commute from his Andheri office, but peaceful and homely. As he headed home to Vasai on July 11, Giribabu died in one of the seven bomb blasts that ripped apart the first class compartments of Western Railway suburban trains. His body was found in Cooper hospital. A starry-eyed software engineer from Nagulapadu village in Guntur district, Giribabu had worked in Hyderabad before coming to Mumbai. For the past year and a half, he'd been working in a division of Polaris Software Lab Ltd, one of the country's top software developers. It was a Mumbai dream for the newly-married couple, but it ended tragically. His wife, still to finish her graduation and able to converse only in Telugu and broken English, was a home-maker. Immediately after the blasts, she moved to her native town near Hyderabad, leaving the home that they had taken on rent about 11 months ago. 'My wife speaks Telugu so she used to spend some time with us,' said an aged neighbour, not wishing to be named. 'We helped her after the blasts because they didn't have anyone here. But they didn't really interact much with the others.' Giribabu was cremated in his native town.

187 MUMBAI LIFE STORIES

Ramzanali Motani

Came from Gujarat, was the family's only earning member

For Mumtaz Motani, the last six months have been hell. Having lost her husband, Ramzanali Motani (51), in the 7/11 serial train blasts, she has been unable to put her mind to anything else. 'Somehow, I can get through the day, but cannot bear the nights,' she says. Born in Rajura village of Gujarat, Ramzanali was the third of six siblings. Both his father, a vegetable-seller, and his mother, a housemaid, realized his inclination towards studies. So they worked very hard to ensure he was educated. After he graduated, Ramzanali decided to head for Mumbai, assuring his worried parents he had friends who would help him get a job. But that was far from the truth. Luckily, he did get work and even went back to his village to get married to Mumtaz. Over the years, Ramzanali brought his siblings to the city. In 1997, he left his job in a timber company to start a family business. But they suffered huge losses in 1999–2000, forcing them to shut down. Most of his family members returned to Rajura, while he joined the Maclay Timber Mart on Grant Road in the accounts department. The Motanis lived simply – Ramzanali loved Kathiawari food of khichdi, bajre ki roti, kadhi etc. As head and the only earning member of the family, he always tried to inculcate a sense of responsibility among his sons. 'He always told us that education and prayers would take us ahead in life,' says son Rafiq. The Motanis have lived through some tough times. During the 1992 riots they were the only Muslims left in Charkop area and had to flee their home, abandoning all their belongings.

Nawalbhai Mathuria

An optician, identified by the dollars he was carrying for his son

That day, Nawalbhai (64) had gone to a meet a friend in south Mumbai to arrange for some foreign exchange for his son who was returning to the US the following day. 'Nawalbhai carried a cell phone and would always call home at intervals of an hour or two,' says his long-time neighbour and relative B.M. Jangla. As news of the blasts reached them, his wife Hansaben, son Pranav and daughter Hemal panicked. They couldn't reach him. After a long search his body was found in JJ hospital. 'His identity card, watch and wallet were missing. Only the dollar bills he was carrying for Pranav were with him, in his shirt pocket. We could identify him only because of those,' says Jangla. The Mathurias came to Jangla Nagar in Malad East in 1968. All 14 residents of Building No 1 are from Saurashtra. Nawalbhai, a succesful optician, liked to keep himself busy. Though he wasn't going to their shop in Borivali these days, he would accompany a friend every day to Chasma Galli near Mangaldas Market to spend time and trade in the city's wholesale market for spectacles. He had agreed to go with him for a few hours saying, '*Ghar baith ke kya karoonga*,' even though wife Hansaben wanted him to spend more time at home with his son who was here only for a short while, and because he was soon going to be a grandfather. While daughter Hemal is an MBBS and lives with her family at the Reliance quarters in Gujarat, son Pranav, who lived in the US, has decided to stay back and move in with his mother.

JIGNESH MEHATA

A cricket fan, celebrated 24th birthday four days earlier

On July 7, 2006 Jignesh Mehata turned 24. Four days later, he died in the blast that ripped apart the first class coach of a Borivali-bound local at Khar station. That day Jignesh Mehata had plans. He was returning home early to take part in a night cricket match organized at his residential complex, Sundaram Co-operative Housing Society in Borivali. 'He was a cricket fan and even fought with his boss to get here early,' says Jayesh Shroff, family friend and neighbour. Soon after graduating in commerce from SIWS College (Wadala), Jignesh wanted to start working. The idea was to contribute to the family's finances. He started as a relationship manager at Sharekhan.com – an online share-trading portal – where he would buy and sell shares on behalf of his clients. 'He was working out of the Sion branch, prior to which he was with a sub-broker who has a Sharekhan franchise,' says Mehul Koradia, who hired him. 'A very shy boy who didn't talk much', is how most colleagues remember him. But, adds Koradia, 'He was very interested in finance and secondary markets.' A video game aficionado, 'Jignesh loved Demo Race, a bike-racing game,' recalls colleague Jaiprakash Singh. 'He didn't know how to drive himself, but loved the sharp turns of the high-speed game.' Singh, who remembers they had both joined the office on the same day in October 2004, enjoyed the lunch-hour feasts they shared in the Himalaya restaurant. He recalls how Jignesh, a Jain and a strict vegetarian, relished kulchas and savoury breads.

187 MUMBAI LIFE STORIES

Prataprai Vora

Came from Gujarat, was in the business of electrical appliances

During the deluge of 2005 the temple on the ground floor of their residential complex was flooded. And when the water receded, Prataprai Vora (75) took it upon himself to collect all the wet currency notes from the donation box and ensure they were cleaned and dried. A Deravasi Jain, Prataprai was deeply religious. He found solace in prayer and was often seen at the beautifully decorated Derasar temple on the ground floor of their housing complex. For the last six months, his family, wife Prabhavati, son Nitin and daughter Harsha have been trying hard to come to terms with what has happened. And prayer is helping them. Neighbour Bharati Soni recollects how Vora would spend endless hours at the temple. 'He would pray at the temple every day. Our colony floods all the time, and he has always helped people.' Originally from Latipur, a sleepy hamlet near Jamnagar in Gujarat, Prataprai bought his 600 square foot flat in Neelkamal Society, a quiet residential complex in Mumbai's western suburb of Kandivali, 20 years ago. Since then, he had been living there, continuing to make a life out of a business in electrical appliances. Prataprai was a home-bird. 'He would pull out a chair onto the verandah of the ground floor as the little children would ride their tricycles in circles around him. He loved to play with them,' says C.H. Parikh, another neighbour, who would often spot him taking a walk late in the evenings. His closest friend, M.K. Doshi, says: 'A couple of days before 7/11, Prataprai told me he was happy that, despite his age, his relatives still thought him useful.'

Sachin Khanna

Company used his initials to brand products

At Sachin Khanna's new residence in Kandivali, there's a plastic cover on the nameplate. Inside the house, white sheets cover the new furniture but can't hide the memories and hopes that are associated with the house; a house they could finally call their own. Sachin Khanna (28) had worked hard for his dream home. A sales manager with Gemini Global, a company dealing in light fixtures, he was an asset to his employers. 'I still remember the Tata Consultancy Services order. We were all working hard to get it,' recalls his colleague and friend Nidhi Hinduja. 'It was a big order for us, but Sachin got it with such ease. He was a genius.' Father-in-law Lalwani says the company was so happy with him for having bagged the Rs 2-crore deal that his bosses actually branded the lights 'Esskay' after him. In fact, Gemini had planned to send him to Bangalore for an exhibition to learn about new light designs and build fresh contacts on July 12. Sachin leaves behind his college sweetheart and wife Kashish and their four-year-old daughter Kanishka who is studying at Malad's Ryan International. 'Their love story was something else,' Lalwani says about his daughter and son-in-law. Last April, the entire family had gone to Kashmir. Coincidentally, it was also their wedding anniversary. 'It is said that love makes people do crazy things. Sachin actually went hunting for pastries and soft drinks at 11 pm to celebrate six years of togetherness.' To Lalwani, Sachin was more than a son. 'It was as if he didn't just marry my daughter, but married the whole family.'

187 MUMBAI LIFE STORIES

Shakir Husain Abdeali Merchant

Lawyer, retired as Chief Metropolitan Magistrate

Ten-year-old Kaisar is waiting to read this story about his grandfather. So here goes: Shakir Husain Abdeali Merchant (72) worshipped work and harboured only one wish: to be able to continue to work till his last breath. Ever since he retired as the Chief Metropolitan Magistrate in 1994, he was practising law in Mumbai courts and continued to do so until 7/11, when he died in the Jogeshwari train blast. Wife of 41 years, Rehana calls him the 'gentleman husband' while daughter Naseem and son Zulfikar don't remember a single instance when he raised his voice. Fellow magistrates and colleagues share similar memories; they say he was disciplined, methodical and straightforward. Shakir and Rehana were Bohra Muslims from Malegaon. 'My father always wanted him as his son-in-law,' smiles Rehana. 'Hard-working, meticulous and systematic. That's how I remember him when we came to Bombay in 1965 and he was a practising lawyer. At home, he was a gentleman. Very tidy.' Daughter Naseem, living with her parents along with her son ever since her divorce, has her own stories about her father. 'He was always calm, I have never seen him angry in my life.' In October 2006 a relative from Pune called Rehana to ask if Shakir had been written about in this series. 'I immediately went to get *The Indian Express* to see what was being written. I liked it so much that, from the next day, we started getting the paper to read about the victims' families,' says Rehana. On many afternoons, she says, these 187 stories lightened her pain, as she realized she wasn't in this alone.

Ashfaq Khan

2008, and the horror continues

Three days after serial blasts shook Jaipur on 13 May, 2008 the nightmare of the equally horrific 7/11 bombings returned to haunt Mumbai. Ashfaq Khan, a railway engineer who was seriously injured in the 2006 commuter train blasts and had since undergone seven brain surgeries, developed fresh complications and died before he could reach hospital, becoming the 188th victim of the Mumbai train blasts. An electrical engineer, Khan (54) had sustained severe head injuries and was in a coma for three months after the blasts in 2006, before showing some signs of improvement. The father of twin girls he was partially paralyzed and suffered acute memory loss before losing the battle for his life. In January, 2008 he was operated on and a plastic flap fixed on the right side of his badly injured skull. 'He was okay after the operation and was regularly taking his medicines,' his wife Rubina says, adding that he would get seizures sometimes. 'He had an attack at 4 this morning and we were taking him to a hospital near our house but he didn't make it...' her voice trails off. Khan was in the first class compartment of a Borivali local when a blast ripped through it on the evening of July 11, 2006, near the Santa Cruz station. 'He was not the same person after the blasts,' says Rubina, wiping the tears off her face. 'His face was badly damaged and sometimes he forgot me and the house but he never forgot our twins, Sadaf and Saman. He wanted to get them to study as much as they could.' Rubina says now she has no idea how she will fulfil her husband's dream.

Investigations

Y.P. Rajesh

It's a lament often heard from police and security officials around the world: terrorists need to be lucky just once to strike their target; those trying to stop them have to be lucky every single time. India, by that yardstick, has had more than its share of bad luck. While the country has been bled by itinerant insurgencies in its remote northeast for decades, the true face of terrorism hit home in the 1980s when Sikh separatist militants in the northern state of Punjab launched a campaign for an independent homeland. Another separatist movement in the Himalayan region of Jammu and Kashmir, which began in 1989, saw an escalation in the levels of mindless violence, which then flowed gradually into the hinterland. Landmines, transistor bombs, random raids by gunmen, hijackings, hostage crises and even suicide attacks have been a part of the Indian vocabulary for over two decades now. Mumbai, the buzzing commercial and entertainment nerve centre of the nation, has also had its share of horrors, with the 1993 serial bomb blasts which killed 257 people standing out as India's worst terror attack. Yet, it would not be an understatement to say that the overcrowded metropolis, or for that matter, the country, was not adequately prepared to prevent 7/11 or tackle its aftermath.

The targeting of the city's overground commuter train network – the rickety lifeline of six million people – as thousands rushed home from work on a monsoon evening was as diabolic as a plot could get. Seven bombs, all placed inside packed coaches – a metaphor for overcrowding during rush hour –

killed 187 people and injured more than 800 within a matter of minutes on seven trains at different points on the network. The chaotic nature of the target also meant that investigating the attacks would be one of the toughest such jobs faced by the Indian police, if not the toughest.

The crime scene could not be preserved well enough for forensic experts to gather as many clues as they could, due to the haphazard rescue efforts by passengers, heavy rain, and the fact that the damaged coaches were removed overnight and train services restored the next morning to send the signal that Mumbai would not be stopped in its tracks.

The Anti-Terrorism Squad (ATS) of Maharashtra, the western Indian state of which Mumbai is the capital, was given the task of investigating the attacks and was assisted by forensic and explosives experts from around the country. The damaged coaches were removed to special areas as detectives searched them for clues about the nature of the explosives used; signatures, if any, of the group behind the operation. And they sieved every bit of information. A technical analysis team analysed hundreds of thousands of phone calls, looking for that one piece of information that would provide a lead to the attackers; spot that one oversight that would blow their cover.

The first conclusion the investigators came to, based on clues they picked up from the crime scene and the disjointed titbits of intelligence they had amassed about the run-up to the attacks, was that this was yet another manifestation of pan-Islamic radicalism. Over the years, Indian cities have increasingly become a target of Islamist militant groups operating in Kashmir and collaborating with their counterparts in neighbouring Pakistan as well as Bangladesh. Indian authorities have for long believed, often with good reason, that most of these groups are backed by Pakistan's subversive military spy agency, the Inter-Services Intelligence or ISI, for a range of historic, political and strategic reasons.

Six months before the Mumbai attacks, the ATS had busted a group of Kashmiri men in Maharashtra who were carrying electronic devices that could be used in explosives and had learnt that another such group was on its way. Two months before the blasts, a large quantity of arms was seized from a group of men suspected by the investigators to belong to the outlawed Students Islamic Movement of India (SIMI) from another part of Maharashtra. But these cases had not yielded enough evidence to prevent the train attacks or pinpoint its perpetrators.

The first big lead came from tracking telephone conversations. A call from a man in Mumbai to a village on India's border with Nepal talking about the blasts, led to the first significant arrest. The suspect was a man from that village. The information provided by him led to more suspects being rounded up from Mumbai and elsewhere. Many of them were suspected SIMI activists or supporters, thereby lending credence to the investigators' theory that Islamist militant groups in Pakistan may have moved on from executing attacks in India themselves, to building a base of disaffected Indians to do it for them. Whatever their allegiance, finding them was a humongous task for the investigators.

Some of the most crucial breakthroughs in the case came due to the ingenuity of the interrogators as well as plain and simple luck. The arrest of the man on the Nepal border had led to the arrest of another 11 men. The first big breakthrough subsequently came when some of the accused were put through a narco test – a process in which suspects are medically administered barbiturates or Sodium Pentothal, believed to lower inhibitions, thus letting down their guard enough to truthfully answer questions. Although Indian courts, like many around the world, do not admit information or confessions extracted through this process, investigators in India use them to seek clues that can, in turn, lead them to evidence.

In one instance, in this investigation, one suspect who had undergone a narco test and one who hadn't were both put in the same room and the one who had not been tested was curious to know how it worked. The other ended up giving him not just details of the narco test but also exchanging notes about the attack, corroborating what the investigators wanted to know and naming another suspect.

What the two men did not realize was that the Anti-Terrorism Squad had done something as simple as bugging the cell. Their entire conversation was recorded, leading to the arrest of the 13th man from Hyderabad city.

Using another classic interrogation technique, ATS officers threw pictures of children killed in the mosque bomb blasts in Malegaon town in Maharashtra – which came two months after 7/11 – on the face of one of the arrested men as they questioned him. He was then asked if this is what jihad was meant to achieve. The killing of innocent young children? Is that what Islam preached? He was asked if he had children of his own, and when he replied in the affirmative, officers told him that, one day, they too could end up being the victims of such attacks. The man broke down and ended up providing vital information.

In other methods used, the suspects were asked the same questions countless times by different officers, their answers recorded on video each time and studied by experts for changes in body language, and for any contradictions in their answers. The 'confessions' of the suspects – made under a stringent anti-terror law which allows this to be admitted in court and prevents the suspect from withdrawing it – allowed Mumbai Police to claim that they had cracked the case in less than three months.

The whole attack, Mumbai Police concluded, was planned by Pakistan's ISI and carried out by the Islamist militant group Lashkar-e-Toiba and its operatives in India. They believe that at least 30 men were involved in the bombings. While 13 Indians were arrested, one suspected Pakistani man was killed in the blasts, another was shot dead in a gun battle with Mumbai Police, and the rest are fugitives in India or have returned to Pakistan. Many of the Indian suspects, Mumbai Police alleges, were trained in Pakistan. According to their investigative team, the RDX explosives to make the bombs were brought to Mumbai by one of the Pakistani men and kept in pressure cookers, placed inside bags, and covered with newspapers or umbrellas after being left to explode through timers. While charges were framed about a year after the blasts and the trial has started, the 13 accused have refused to plead either guilty or not guilty.

Besides this, some of them have sought translators, some others have excused their lawyers from representing them, and some have even asked for a new judge saying the serving one does not inspire confidence – all of which has slowed down the trial. In March 2008, four months before the second anniversary of the blasts, the Supreme Court stopped the trial as a bench agreed to examine the constitutional validity of a specific part of the anti-terror law MCOCA (Maharashtra Control of Crime Act) that refers to 'insurgency', after it was questioned by one of the 13 accused.

Mumbai Police believes that the accused could be adopting a strategy to delay the trial in an attempt to gradually turn the tide in their favour, or at least to blunt the prosecution's case. As the trial gets prolonged, the sense of involvement and the commitment of officers and witnesses is known to get diluted. Memories fail and fatigue sets in. Whenever the trial resumes, it is expected to take about a year to be completed and though the prosecution believes it has a strong case based on 'evidence and logic', they have few hopes of getting to the fugitives as Pakistan, like in the past, has not shown any inclination to help find them despite repeated pleas.

Some legal experts, however, feel that the prosecution's case rests largely on circumstantial evidence and confessional statements made in custody and is not as watertight as believed. Questions have also been raised about the exact roles of many of the accused, with some critics saying that most of them played only peripheral parts in the attacks.

Clearly, the 7/11 trial could end up being as tortuous as the investigations and in the end, might still leave some questions unanswered.

Hope Keeps Them Going

Jinal Shah

'Parag, *baba kuthe aahe*?' asks his mother and the 28-year-old's eyes search for his father, hiding in the corner of a curtained enclosure in Hinduja hospital. Both Madhuri and Jaiprakash, parents of Parag Sawant, are trying hard to jog Parag's memory and re-familiarize him with the people he's known all his life. He quickly recognizes his parents and wife but is completely blank when his one-and-a-half-year-old daughter looks at her father and promptly lisps 'Papa' with pride. Both Parag and his daughter Prachiti are on the same level; graduating at the same pace. And poised between the two of them, is a family praying that one day Parag will recognize his child.

'He shakes hands, raises his fingers in order from thumb to last finger. On New Year's Eve, when one of his brothers was eating a Cadbury's chocolate in front of him he opened his mouth, as he was tempted to have it. Like Prachiti, he will refuse to get out of bed for a bath in winter. He smiles when he listens to music. He boxes with nurses if they tease him that Sushma is not his wife,' says his mother.

The Mumbai blasts of 2006 devastated more then a thousand families. For some of those who weren't killed outright, the agony has not ceased. Among the countless afflicted, for whom Black Tuesday is frozen in time, are the Sawants.

Parag has sustained severe injuries to his head. The doctors have almost given up on him and predict that he might well be like this all his life. Still, even though he is in a semi-comatose condition, Parag's family has not given up hope. They are valiantly battling the terrible outcome of 11 July 2006 to this day.

'Now on Ganpati we just pray for Parag's health,' says Jaiprakash. Parag's father works as a welder at Mazgaon dock. He still travels in trains every day from his Bhayander residence to the hospital and to work. 'It was fated to happen,' he says. 'We are not well off, and the trains are our only mode of transport, so we have to be resilient,' he adds. These days the family is busy finalizing the colour they want to paint their house. 'Just before the blasts, Parag had called me and asked that all family members be present at home to select the colour. Since that day we are still waiting for him to instruct us on the colour. We took up the painting work only recently as we want to welcome him home to a freshly painted house,' says his mother with a catch in her voice.

A few kilometres away, in the high-dependency unit at Jaslok hospital, 22-year-old Amit Singh lies listlessly, his arms and legs frozen, his eyes refusing to recognize anyone apart from the members of his immediate family. He drifted into this semi-comatose state soon after the blast at Mira Road. Two years after the terrible incident, this passionate volleyball player shows no sign of improvement.

His father believes that if a doctor from a developed country took up his son's case and treated him with new medicines and the latest technology he might improve. 'I am even ready to give my son for research. Doctors here have given their 100 per cent but have not found a solution yet.' Singh resolutely refuses to give up and continues to run from hospital to hospital, showing his son's medical reports and consulting with doctors. 'I've shown his reports to all the top doctors in Mumbai's hospitals.' But Dinesh Singh has faced dejection everywhere.

Amit's eyes, like those of Parag's, flicker for a split second as if in comprehension, but the very next moment turn listless again.

For the last 24 months, the Singh and Sawant families have made the hospital their home. Parag, who became a father one-and-a-half years ago has no clue that he is a parent and doesn't bat an eyelid when his daughter, Prachiti is put on his lap.

Amit, whose B. Com results were declared after the blasts, secured a first class, though he remains oblivious to the fact. He has turned two years older lying in the same hospital but everything else in his life is in stasis.

Both families had little in common before the blast. Now it's the tragedy of their sons' lives that has brought them together. Or, perhaps, more than the tragedy, it's the tiny sliver of hope – of one day seeing their sons walk out of the hospital – that they share.

Learning to Cope

Kavitha Iyer

A picnic or a movie afternoon with the '7/11 group' is one of the things that psychologist and counsellor Meeta Shah is looking forward to. It has been ten months now since they first met at her suburban apartment and the women have been busy. Some are juggling their single mother status with their first job, others have teenage children whose academics – school and university exams, competitive exams for an entry into premier higher education institutes and professional courses – render home schedules hectic.

But with two years gone since Meeta lost her husband Tushit Shah to a bomb explosion aboard a local train, she wants the women left behind by the serial explosions – soul sisters tied by some ethereal thread – to meet once again. She is hoping also that more women get to know of this group, and come forward to comfort and to be comforted. 'Sharing helps. I just want us to be with one another, to give strength and get strength so we don't lose our courage to stand alone in tough situations.'

At 45, Meeta misses the romance in her kitchen and the endless silly jokes at home. Intermittently, she is besieged by guilt, for instance when she realizes that she hasn't shared a hearty laugh with her kids in a long, long time. At such moments, she frets about whether she has been a good mother to her children.

'Not one moment passes, happy or sad, when I don't miss him,' she says, adding that wounds don't ever heal, though time dulls the trauma. 'So you learn to move on. Your kids rely on you, so you tell yourself to be less selfish, show less self pity.'

Her daughter, Esha, aspiring to be a biotechnologist, keeps Meeta firmly grounded in the present. From chiding her for an unfashionable outfit – 'Would Papa have liked you to dress like this?' – to spurring her to be positive, Esha nudges her mother closer to the person she was before tragedy struck.

It was, in part, a sense of gratitude for all the support she was receiving from friends and family that led Meeta to want to reach out to the other women suffering the same anguish she felt. Then, when she heard that the widows of 7/11 were finding it difficult to find employment commensurate with their qualifications, Meeta got together with four or five other women and wrote a letter to the Union Railway Ministry, New Delhi. 'Nothing came of that, though.'

Still, an idea had developed – that they could talk to each other, because they understood each other's plight. They met at her home less than a year ago, maybe ten or twelve of them. They chatted, somebody mentioned that one woman had married again. 'I was happy to hear that. Our society, even in a city like Mumbai, can be so conservative sometimes,' Meeta says.

A few counsellor friends pitched in next for a small drawing session for the kids. 'We wanted to motivate them through art. Psychology and art are deeply interconnected, I enjoy dealing with children through art,' she says. 'But this didn't work out that well. Not too many people knew we were doing something like this, I guess.' Of course, all the women from the families of the victims haven't met one another. But those who have, keep in touch. They meet at various occasions, some at an Art of Living workshop organized for post-7/11 trauma victims, others at a session chaired by a well-known psychiatrist. Still others meet at work, having accepted employment with Western Railway, on whose trains the carnage had played out.

On every occasion, the women quietly exchange numbers.

At the Railway Accidents Claims' Tribunal, which heard individual cases before awarding compensation to victims' families, Sunita Kewat met Sunita Pawar, both 7/11 widows. Several months later, when they met again at a function, Mrs Kewat thrust her telephone number in the other Sunita's palm. 'You have to start talking to people,' she told the visibly withdrawn Pawar, speaking in their native language, Marathi. With Kewat was Prawara Patil, another 7/11 widow. 'Prawara and I also met at the tribunal, you know,' Kewat told Pawar.

Pawar later accepted a job at the tribunal offices, a gruelling 100-minute commute from her home in Gorai, a far-flung suburb, 'the last bus-stop' of the city transport undertaking. Over the months, the two Sunitas have become fast friends, confidantes, 'like sisters', sharing everything from dilemmas over finances to child-rearing predicaments, the latter being an area of concern for almost every family bereaved by 7/11.

To Meeta's great pleasure, her daughter Esha has learnt to wring out some positive from the worst circumstances. 'She wants to promote peace,' says the proud mother. 'She asks me often why people quarrel, why they're so negative. She avoids meeting people who are negative, and always thanks God for not putting in her the vindictiveness and anger she sees in others.'

On the evening of May 13, 2008 when Meeta switched on the television and found news breaking of serial bomb blasts in the tourist city of Jaipur, the capital of the desert state of Rajasthan, Esha reached for the remote control. 'We don't want to watch this, Mama,' she told Meeta. 'We have suffered this. What more can we see that we don't already know?'

Preparing frantically for a series of entrance exams to engineering courses in institutes across the country, Esha has had a busy summer, keeping Meeta busy with ferrying her to classes, getting various documents ready to be dispatched with admission forms, and accompanying her daughter to examination centres.

Esha is keen to study biotechnology and environmental sciences. But the teenager now suffers severe migraines, a new reaction to stress and tension.

'The 7/11 children I met were all affected in some way or another,' says Minal Lonkar-Kavishwar, whose Pune-based NGO Animal Angels contacted the Bombay Psychiatric Society a few months after the blasts.

A certified animal therapist with over five years of documented research, she despatched to them articles from foreign newspapers detailing how trained animals had assisted in relief operations after 9/11 and, more recently, Hurricane Katrina. In December 2006, Lonkar-Kavishwar addressed doctors, survivors and the kin of those who'd died in the blasts, describing her work with volunteer-dogs and children with autism, learning disabilities and physical disabilities. 'Just telling children to be brave was not going to be enough, that was clear.'

Meeta has been reading self-help books on positive thinking; has shifted residence 'just for a change'; and has made a conscious effort to go out regularly and meet people. Still, she sometimes wakes up in the middle of the night, sobbing and weeping, after a recurring nightmare that her husband is not dead, but alive, somewhere around, unable to contact his loved ones.

In a cold sweat, she asks herself each time if, given a choice, Tushit would have left them, and then answers the question herself: 'Never.'

And that thought gives her strength.

Maximum City

Farah Baria

As usual, it's an entire country in a railway compartment.

There's a south Indian matriarch combing her frizzy hair, two Gujarati hausfraus swapping recipes at full volume, an incognito woman in a black burka snoring gently, a prostitute from Kamathipura in a bright orange salwar kameez and matching lipstick, a Punjabi lady industriously writing her Ram Naam in a dog-eared notebook, and a Maharashtrian stenographer chopping carrots into a little plastic bag for dinner. Sisters and strangers, united by the journey of life on a Mumbai train.

At the far end, I spy three teenagers, ethnically unidentifiable in jeans and tee-shirts. They are haggling over two-rupee hairclips with a grimy, five-year-old vendor wearing a discarded party frock, and a smile worth a million bucks.

At the door is the sentry: an old beggar with stumps for legs, the only male permitted in this jealously guarded female bogey. Beyond the chicken mesh that respectably separates the 'leddies logh' from male eyes, you can hear a standing Bhajan Group, noisily praising the Lord to the steady clash of cymbals, and the clackety-clack of train wheels.

Seated next to them is the Patta gang, deftly sorting their decks on briefcase-top card tables. And, at the rain-drenched window, the Dalal Street set argues amiably with the diamond merchants' clique, on the relative merits of Reliance versus Infosys. Obviously, it's something they have argued about for years.

But things aren't quite this civilized before departure.

When the empty Virar Fast pulls slowly into Churchgate station at peak hour today, it is seized, captured and annexed by 5000 edgy predators, desperately preying on less than 2000 seats.

Push, shove, scramble, grab. You know how it is in the urban jungle: only the fittest survive. Regular pass-holders are grudgingly awarded the prime window seats, like regal lions after the kill. Other scavengers settle for less plum positions next to crowded gangways. And the meek inherit the exits until they are disgorged at their destinations. Then, almost miraculously, when the ranks have settled and the wheels start to click, competition turns to camaraderie, and belligerence to amiable chit-chat. (Hey, what's a little squabbling between friends?)

It's a muggy, malodorous, asphyxiating ride on a 60 kilometre track that cleaves through the island of Mumbai, like a knife slicing through a piquant chilli. The heavily barred windows are secured with chicken mesh, the smell of rusting iron seeps into your skin, the seats are hard and unforgiving, and the grating fans try valiantly to stir the stale air.

No frills here, just the bare bones of civic amenities, minus the bare basics of human dignity. And yet, like thousands of my fellow citizens, I love these tired old trolleys that hurtle through good times and bad. The reason is simple.

Mumbai's trains connect me with my country, both literally and figuratively. They are India in microcosm, diverse, yet united by aspiration. Competitive, yet strangely content.

Aggressive, yet accepting. Parochial, yet secular. Chaotic, yet orderly. Crowded and shabby, but intent on racing into the future on the engine of Hope.

It is this precious hope that the bombs tried to destroy.

And precisely the reason why Mumbai's trains will never stop running.

INDEX

ACKNOWLEDGEMENTS

Thanks are due to The Indian Express Team in Mumbai, including Shantanu Datta, Akella Srinivas, Mahendra Parikh, Vasant Prabhu, Kevin D'souza, Ashish Shankar, Pradip Das, Prashant Nadkar,Ganesh Shirsekar,Pradeep Kochrekar, Dilip Kagda, Neeraj Priyadarshi, Swatee Kher, Smita Nair, Jinal Shah, N Ganesh , Kalpana Verma, Kavitha Iyer, Swapnil Rawal, Mohan Kumar, Prashant Rangnekar, Sudheendra Tripathi, Lekha Agarwal, Sayli Udas, Menaka Rao, Mihika Basu, Anumeha Yadav, Chitrangada Chowdhury, Ashutosh Patil, Bhushan Shinde, Divya Sama, Jaya Menon, Aparna Chandra, Sulakshana Gupta, Mitali Kalyanpur, Amit Sharma, Ayesha Khan, Triveni Rangarajan, Farah Baria & Y.P. Rajesh.

The Indian Express Team in New Delhi, including Rajkamal Jha, Unni Rajen Shanker, Seema Chishti, Ambreen Khan & Pankaj Bhutani.

We would also like to thank HarperCollins Publishers Ltd. and Krishan Chopra & Nandita Aggarwal for their interest in this project.